John T. Beer

The Prodigal

A dramatic poem

John T. Beer

The Prodigal
A dramatic poem

ISBN/EAN: 9783337036713

Printed in Europe, USA, Canada, Australia, Japan

Cover: Foto ©Thomas Meinert / pixelio.de

More available books at **www.hansebooks.com**

THE PRODIGAL;

A Dramatic Poem.

BY

JOHN T. BEER,

AUTHOR OF "MISCELLANEOUS POEMS."

I was—I am—but O, what shall I be?

Page 90.

LONDON:
PETER DOW, BREAD STREET HILL.

1861.

INTRODUCTION.

The kind and liberal reception given to my former Volume of Poems, by a very numerous circle of Friends and Patrons, has encouraged me to redeem the promise made in the introduction connected therewith.

Conscious of many defects in the accompanying Poem, it is with much diffidence, that I now present it to the indulgence of those whose previous kindness has earned my utmost confidence.

My one excuse for the many faults, which are sure to be detected by the critical reader, is this, that commercial engagements, leave me but little time, for the study or cultivation of poetical composition, or ideas.

If asked, why, under such circumstances, I venture to trespass upon the sacred and exclusive domain of Poetry; I reply, that in so doing

I pleasure my own mind, and breathe an atmosphere congenial to my soul.

The novel enterprise connected with the distribution of these works, having fulfilled my largest expectations, I take this opportunity of thanking my many Friends for their obliging favours; and to assure them of my constant devotion to their interest, while labouring to promote my own.

If the perusal of this book should convey pleasure or profit to any, and lead to a more careful and thoughtful study of that sublime parable upon which it is founded, I shall reap a perfect recompence for the years of labour, of which this feeble production has been the object.

The conditions of distribution, are the same as on former occasions,—viz.—Purchasers of Goods, to the amount of One Pound or upwards, will be entitled to receive One Copy.

JOHN T. BEER.

32, Briggate, Leeds,
April 1st, 1861.

THE PRODIGAL.

PART I.—Scene I.

The Garden of a Mansion in the Suburbs of Jerusalem. Evening. Enter Haden and Hamel.

Haden.

BUT why, my son, art thou resolved to leave
Thy home, thy kindred, and this sacred land,
Which God to our forefathers did bequeath
In a perpetual grant? A land that flows
With wine and milk and oil; honey and corn;
Whose very stones are iron, and from whose hills,
Thou may'st dig brass. Where God bestows,
From the full hand of His beneficence,
All He has promised, and our needs require.
Dost thou so lightly view the glorious boon
Of thy exalted birthright as a Jew,
As to despise the land that gave thee birth?

This Queen of lands, bright Palestine the Fair.
This holy soil, that bears through all its length
The footprints of our God: where He has shewn
His glory to our race, and in their sight,
Made bare His wonder-working arm. And who,
In thunders, has proclaimed His sov'reign law.
A land of marvels, prophets, miracles;
Whose every hill stands forth a monument:
And all its vales His praise and glory sing.
Hast thou not read, and have not I declared,
Those glorious archives of our nation's rise,
Since first our Syrian father wandered out
A stranger from his home, to what became
A land of promise to his future seed,
When he as yet, both childless was and old?
And how the promise was confirmèd by
A child of age, when in the usual course
Of nature, such was thought impossible?
And how the fathers of our tribes were led,
With Israel at their head, to sojourn long
In Egypt's treach'rous land? which soon became
A house of bondage, slavery, and woe;
Till their united bitter cry went up
In such a wail of lamentation, as

Prevailed on God to vindicate their cause,
And execute His vengeance on their foes,
In many fearful plagues; until their wail,
Exceeded even that which had been wrung
From Israel's helpless ones. A deathly wail !
Such as before, or since, was never heard,
Since God destroyed the old rebellious world
In seas of wrath. And how they instant bade,
Our fathers fly from thence with earnest haste,
O'erladen with their gifts, a lawful spoil,
For service still unpaid, and woes endured ?
How next He clave the watery deep in twain,
And reared it up as ramparts right and left,
A passage for their tribes; who marchèd through
The sea as on dry land: which swallowed up,
In its relentless grasp, proud Pharaoh and his host ?
A godless army, who, in wrathful pride,
Close followed in the steps of those whom God
Had saved by miracle; thus did they bring
A swift destruction from the vengeful arm
Of Heaven's insulted grace. And how He led,
His people forty years through all the way
Of that great wilderness; and sent them food,
Direct from His own hand; a heavenly feast,

Of such as angels eat ? And water from
The dry and flinty rock; which gushing came
In streams that followed whereso'er they went ?
And how He mapp'd their long uncertain route,
With a display of His own glory, which,
By day in cloud, and by the night in fire,
Traced all their wanderings ? until He gave
The long-desired command, to enter in
To this good land, where Abraham's feet had trod,
And he received in promise from his God.
And how He drave their foes before their face;
And gave them victory o'er those dreaded ones,
The mighty sons of Anak ? men of old
Renowned for deeds of war; in stature vast,
And giants in their strength: yet could they not,
Withstand the potent arm our God displayed,
But were compelled to yield their land and lives
To His Almightiness. And with them fell
Each weaker nation, though the weak were strong,
In walled cities, and in warlike ways.
But God did wage th' exterminating war,
Till Jebusite, and Hivite, and Hittite,
And Perizzite were slain; and all the word
Of promise was fulfilled; and this fair land,

Became for ever our unquestioned home.
And, now, my Hamel, look from where we stand,
On yonder scene, Jehoshaphat's dark vale.
The sun has cast his shadows o'er the tombs,
Where sleep the silent dead, waiting in hope
The great Archangel's summons from the grave.
There lie interred our sires, through a long line
Of noble, honoured names, unbroken thus,—
Except by Chaldea's seventy years of woe,—
Since David first established on the hill,
His heaven-appointed, and most glorious throne.
And I would still preserve intact, the roll
Of our ancestral names, among the dead.
Nor can I hope much longer to remain
A stranger to the dust; but I do hope,
With earnest strong desire, that when my God
Shall call my soul away, my bones may mix
Their earthy clay with my forefathers' soil,
And fain I would my sons should thus fulfil
My latest wish, and with their hands consign
My cold remains to their corrupting home.
Then stay, my boy, where God has fix'd thy lot;
For thou wilt never find in all the earth,
Another land, so fertile, or so fair,

Or half so rich in legendary lore :
Nor where the finger of the living God,
Has writ so many letters of His name,
To make His glory, and His nature known.

Hamel.

I pray my father, that thy honoured head
May long be shielded from the icy grasp
Of stern and merciless death : and that the tomb,
Of those who gave us birth, may long be sealed,
Ere it receives thy patriarchal form.
Ere that transpires, I shall to thee return
Full of the wonders of those distant lands,
Which now I am impatient to behold:
And will recount in thy delighted ears,
All I have learned, and my glad eyes have seen.
I do admit our Palestine is fair;
Its hills vine-covered, and its fruitful vales
Rich in luxuriant waving fields of corn.
While David's City on yon lofty hill,—
Whose gilded spires, reflect the fiery rays
Of heaven's declining sun; and gleam mid-air
Like a bright fortress wrought of burnished gold
By angel-hands, and pois'd 'twixt earth and heaven,—

Must ever claim a song of loudest praise.
And hard indeed, would be my flinty heart,
Could it remain insensible to love
For this our nation, and our nation's pride,
Jerusalem the Grand.   No matter where
From this renownèd spot my feet may roam;
My heart shall stay, and hover round its heights;
And, like a bird, shall build its nest upon
The loftiest pinnacle.   But father hear!
Although I love the land where God has wrought
So many wonders for His chosen race;
And all those wonders on my brain are writ,
As with a pen of fire; yet, does that not
Extinguish from my breast this fix'd desire
To visit other lands, their wonders know;
Read all their history; study all their laws;
And search the mystery of their many arts;
As represent in Egypt, Greece, and Rome.—
Egypt ! that land of vast, gigantic works ;
Where mighty Sphynx, and towering Pyramids,
And ancient Temples, stand as monuments
Of former greatness; comprehensive mind,
Which here developed its sublimest thoughts
In simple majesty.   There I would learn

Those sealèd words upon her marbles writ
In nature's alphabet. Strange characters!
Those hieroglyphics, which in signs convey
Their nation's history, and her line of Kings.
Their vile religion, battles, laws, and games;
Conquests and victories, and triumphal shows;
From long before the date when Israel served
As bondmen to their race. These shall inspire
In my awaking soul, a quickening love
For ancient classic lore; and kindle there,
Ambition's earnest flame to rise beyond
A mere secluded life,—such as till now
Has been my humble lot,—and stand upon
The pinnacle of fame; and hear the voice
Of loud applauding tongues, to bear me on
To great achievements, and to higher aims.
From thence I'll pass to Greece, that land of song,
Where every form is grace, and every word,
Is breathed in accents of poetic strains,
That wakes a chord of sympathy where'er
It strikes on stranger ears. A land of groves,
Of mountains, cataracts, and woods composed
Of scented myrtle, cassia, and balm;
Which spread their perfume on the buoyant air.

And all luxurious things abound, to feed
The most fastidious and refinèd taste;
And gentle winds from off the deep blue waves
Spread healthful freshness o'er the pleasant land.
And Athens from her lofty hill looks down,
As does a Queen upon her royal sons,
Who represent a warlike, noble race;
Which fought with Alexander in the field,
And conquered all the world.   Great are the works
Of which she justly boasts; Temples, and Gods,
And Halls, and Palaces elaborate;
Grand in conception, style, and ornament:
Each, patterns to the world of perfect art.
And where they worship Mars the god of war,
And that great temple to Diana given
At Ephesus, and all those countless works,
Of Gods, and Shrines: Idols of stone,
Which there are multiplied, to such degree,
As to induce the strange incongruous thought
That all the ancient race by some decree
And mandate of the Gods, were petrified,
And now present the pictured form of life,
Breathless and cold, yet beautiful in death.
Next, that great seat of justice, which the Greek

So proudly boasts, the Areopagus:
Whose fame has reached to this our distant land,
I shall survey with my own longing eyes;
While thus as yet, my ears alone have heard
Its praise declared. And father, let me ask,
What's so ennobling, or so well designed
To lift the soul to high and glorious thought,
As contemplation of majestic works,
And great achievements wrought by master minds?
Then leaving Greece with all its vine-clad hills;
Its spicy groves, and foul idolatry;
Its polished sons, still ignorant of God;
I'll pass across the bosom of the deep,
And see the wonders of our glorious God,
Upon the mighty floods. There He displays
His vast sublimity; as wave on wave,
Rolls on unceasingly, with giant strides
O'er all the briny main, unchecked and free.
Or lashed to fierce destructive war, they fly,
Like top'ling mountains down some fearful steep;
Crash upon crash, with wild commotion toss'd;
In surging wrath, and bellowing battle cry;
Till God recalls the wild, unruly blast,
And bids the sea be still. Thence on to Rome!

That city of the west, whose power extends
O'er all the conquered globe. And proudly she
Sits on the banks of Tiber as a Queen;
Empress of nations; mistress of the world.
Whose great renown for wond'rous martial deeds,
Already causes in our nation's breast,
A secret dread of what may henceforth be.
There I shall see the Cæsar in his state;
With all the pomp of high imperial rule,
And all his dazzling panoply of show:
Clad in the gorgeous purple, wrought with gold;
And crowned with diadems. Whose festal board
Groans 'neath the choicest dainties of all lands;
And conquered Kings obsequious serve thereat
As willing slaves; while all her favoured sons
Are free-born princes, whose terrestial lives,
Divide between the strife and din of war,
And soft voluptuousness. There will I dwell;
Behold their state, their wealth, and happiness;
Learn all their laws, and how they frame their codes
To govern realms so vast. Admire their works!
Those lofty columns which commemorate
Their mighty warriors' deeds. The Forum too;
And countless palaces, spread o'er the slopes,

And on the swelling tops of seven hills.
The vast Theatre, Temples, Altars, Gods.
Their martial shows, processions, and reviews:
Their crowned victors, and their mail-clad men;
Those warrior legions, whose all-powerful arms,
Have far and wide, spread terror and dismay.
And may I not, their tactics comprehend,
And art of war? Learn from their practised school,
And treasure up this knowledge, for the day
Of future need? A time not distant far,
When this our country shall shake off the yoke
Of the oppressor's rule, and free herself
From all the stranger's pride. Thus shall I gain,
In these my youthful years, a goodly store
Of knowledge for the need of manhood's prime;
That when the time for our deliverance comes,
I may be found a messenger from God.

Haden.

GOD grant, my son, that no worse cause may flow
From this thy wayward mood; but much I fear,
That thou wilt sooner learn the hateful sins
Of those whom thou would'st know, much rather than
Their doubtful seeming good. And what avail

Would all thy knowledge be, if thou forgot
Him whom thy fathers served, the living God?
And I foresee, as with prophetic gaze,
This dreaded evil pending o'er thy head;
Apostacy from God! than which I would,
Far sooner, even now, submit to lay
Thy lifeless body in sepulchral gloom.
Lift up thine eyes to where on Zion's heights,
The temple of our God conspicuous stands:
The pride of every Jew; the polar star,
To which his eyes from every quarter turn,
Of every land, with feelings most devout.
It is the time of evening sacrifice;
And even now, while thus we do converse,
The holy priest before the altar stands,
And makes atonement with the sprinkled blood
For every soul that sins and does repent.
While earnest prayers escape his quivering lips,
And on the cloud of smoking incense borne
Ascend accepted to our gracious God;
Who condescends his presence to make known
In visible display; which sometimes fills
The house with glory, and the worshippers
With solemn speechless awe.   And where the ark,

Was sacred kept with its appurtenances;
The holy Aaron's rod, that gave forth buds;
The golden pot which held the manna food;
That choice memorial of God's providence:
And over all, with graceful spreading wings,
Cherubic forms were seen, shadowing therewith
The glorious mercy seat, God's earthly throne.
'Tis there our race have ever worshipped Him,
Since first the wise and potent Solomon
Did dedicate the temple to His name,
With seas of blood, and heaven-accepted prayers.
And though that structure by unholy hands
Was part demolished, when the Chaldean King
Led all the princes of our sacred tribes
To Babylon's distant land; yet, was it reared
With earnest zeal again, when there returned
A remnant from their chains. Not like the first
In decorative art, or costly style,
Or grand accompaniment:—yea, so beneath,
That those who called to mind the former shrine,
Wept out their grief at what they now beheld;—
Yet still the house and temple of our God.
And would'st thou fly from where thy God is known?
And where thy fathers offered Him their praise?

And where atonement is unceasing made
For all our nation's guilt, to heathen lands?
Where gross idolatry, and pagan forms,
And rites abominable prevail; and He
Who made the earth, the seas, and heavenly worlds,
Is neither served or known? Wilt thou defile
Thyself with such as these? Eat at their board,
And join their sinful ways; and bring at last
Thyself to ruin, and thy father's head
To a dishonoured grave?

Hamel.

Stay there, my sire!
I should abhor myself, and deem I were
Unworthy of thy name, if I could bring
Such foul discredit on thy ripening years,
And hold to shame, before the jealous eyes
Of all our kindred, thee, my father dear.
Fear not for me; I love our Zion's walls,
Her ritual, and her types; her altars, Priests;
Her feasts, and fasts, and forms: for thou hast taught
Me from my earliest youth, and in thy life
Hast lived the lesson out, of love to her.
And it 's become a settled principle,

Deep rooted in my soul; which all the show
Of Pagan idol pomp; or, all the forms
Of learned sophistry; or, all the vain
Enticements of the world, can ne'er remove.
So far, my father, hath thy anxious care
Led thee to error, as, that I shall grow
But stronger in my faith, when I compare
The worship of our God with that of those,
Who are no gods at all: whose priests are base;
And whose great temples are but dens of crime,
And lewd, unholy spots, where all that's pure
Is banishèd away. No; I will turn
My face to where she sits, at every hour,
Prescribed for holy prayer. Morn, noon, and night,
My spirit shall engage in acts devout,
And hold communion with our Israel's God.
Thus, though removed by intervening space,
Of hills and valleys; deserts, nations, seas;
I shall remain in spirit with my home;
While all the charm Jerusalem inspires,
And all the fond associations, which,
As clustering vines, do gather round her heights,
Shall still abide; and in my soul maintain
A chief supremacy. So shall the germ

Of heaven-engendered life, shoot forth its roots,
And spread its branches wide, and bring forth fruit;
As do the olives on our native hill.

Haden.

Yet, hear me, Hamel, while I further urge
Upon thy hopeful mind another plea;
The plea of love : this should, methinks, prevail,
To turn thee from this folly of thy youth.
Have I not loved thee as a father should;
Borne with thy failings, pitied all thy faults,
And watched with anxious eyes thy upward growth
From infancy till now? Have I not taught,—
As Moses gave command,—the words of truth,
Both in the house and walking by the way ?
Is there a duty which a child demands
From those who gave him life, I have not held
As sacred to perform ? Thou art my last,
My best belovèd son; and on thy youth,
My heart has dwelt with fond complacency;
As by progressive steps, thou hast attained,
To manhood's ripening years; and I have felt,
In all the fulness of a father's love,
A father's pride, which only did behold

The brightest side of that it looked upon.
I have invested thee with every charm
Of innocence and truth, and looked to see
The bud of promise in the full-blown flower.
Shall these, my brightest hopes,—hopes which have
    lain
Hid, like the brilliant jewels of the earth,
In the dark chambers of my secret heart,
Till they should be by thy industrious hand
Brought forth to light,—ne'er find embodiment?
Tell me, my son, if thou can'st thus requite,
With base ingratitude, the love I bear
Unchanged to thee? Why art thou thus resolved
To cast a cloud of sorrow o'er the home,
Where the bright sun of unbeclouded love
Has ever constant shone? My son! my son!
Is there not left one spark of childhood's love?
One tender feeling for thy parent, who
Hath lavishèd such teeming floods on thee
With pure unselfishness? It cannot be,
That thou shouldst thus repay, love with indifference.
I fain would hope of thee much better things,
Than what my fearful heart prognosticates.
Thou wilt not rend those sweet domestic bonds

That round our home are twined; those boons of
    heaven,
Which God in goodness gives to bless our lives,
And kindle in our souls loud songs of praise.
I cannot think that thou with ruthless hand,
Wilt take and scatter to the winds of heaven
Our treasured joys; and open up besides,
The floodgates of such overwhelming grief,
As to imperil every source of joy.

Hamel.

Oh, cease, my father, thus to heap on me,
These keen invectives; for, they rend my soul
With fearful agonies, as carrion birds
Tear piece by piece from off the quivering flesh,
Of the still conscious, unresisting prey.
Think not that I despise or underrate,
The fond affection thou hast ever shown
For me, though so unworthy of thy love.
I have returned but feebly, I will own,
All that thou hast bestowed: it were a task,
Beyond my tender years, to pay in full,
What thou so large hast given. Yet still I love,
With all the filial fondness of a child,

That clings with trusting faith where it has fix'd
Its first affections: so my heart is fix'd;
Nor love of travel, change, the world, or self,
Can ever from my deepest heart destroy
That love for thee. But this does not absorb
All other feelings, nor prevent the course
Of kindred streams that do accord therewith.
And in this settled purpose of my mind,
I can discern nought that does stand opposed
To love of nation, love of God, or thee.
I do presume that these may all remain
Intact and perfect, though my feet may roam
In every foreign land. Then cease to doubt;
Thy doubts are all unjust; and in my soul
Conflicting passions raise, that I would keep
Restrained within myself. It is not well
The sorrows thou dost fear should enter in
The hallowed precincts of our peaceful home;
It need not be! My love will still remain
As warm and ardent as when first it flowed
With undivided childlike faith to thee.
Then give me, father, what my soul most needs,
Thy parting blessing: lay upon my head
Thy hand, and say, " My peace go with thee, son."

Then will my heart be glad, and every joy
Receive a tenfold value in the boon,
Which in my heart of hearts shall treasured lie,
My best inheritance.

Haden.

It cannot be!
Thou dost presume upon my weakness, son,
With oily words, and plausible display
Of flattering speech; anon forgetting, that
Obedience is the duty of the child.
I would have waived this argument, and led
Thee by those gentler means which I have used,
To join accord with my expressed desires:
But since in vain all softer reason fails,
Upon thy hardened ear, this must be used.
Thou art my son; and, as a son, dost owe
Implicit homage to my every word:
For such is God's command, and such have men
In every age endorsed; 'tis nature's law!
If thou didst love me, as thou dost profess,
Thou would'st, with willing heart, obedient prove
To these my just commands. For thou hast read
What holy Samuel says, that God requires

Before e'en sacrifice, *obedience;*
And, rather than burnt offerings, active love.
And I would ask, that thou shouldst rather prove
Thy large professions of unchanging love,
By willing deeds, and sacrifice of self;
In which alone true love is manifest.
I would not pain thine ear, by calling up
In all their various forms, the arguments
Of curses; which, against rebellious sons
Are hurled as bolts of fire, from the high hand
Of heaven's avenging God. Thou knowst them well,
And shouldst, methinks, be moved to contemplate
This wild, unhallowed mood, and not to rush
Upon the judgments of our jealous God,
As does the thoughtless steed, with snorting breath,
Dash heedless on 'midst war's destructive din.
Thou wilt assuredly bring Heaven's vengeance down—
A sword of judgment on thy naked head,
And where no hand of mine can interpose
To ward the dreadful blow: or to thy wants,—
Which like strange spectres shall around thee rise,
And grin their fiendish malice in thy face,—
One jot administer. Then pause my son!
Thy inclination now supremely rules

O'er all thy better judgment; and its chains
Hold wisdom, prudence, reason, closely bound;
While duty lies within thy hardening breast
A smothered fire, whose embers scarcely shew
One spark of life. Its voice was often heard
In tones of warning, counsel, and advice,
Till all unheeded it has ceased to speak;
Except in dark, ambiguous, feeble sounds,
Like some dull murmur rising from the grave.
Then heed me, boy, ere it shall be too late;
Revive the spark to pristine brilliancy;
Arouse thyself to catch the murmured tones;
Till treasured, and encouraged, they return
With all their former frequency and power,
To guide thy actions right; for duty's path,
Of every other way in which we walk,
Is only safely trod. And when we leave
This for the world's bye-ways, we fly from God.
Thus heretofore I have entreated thee
With friendship's earnestness: now, I do command
Thee, as thy lawful Sire, " Thou must not go."

Hamel.

It grieves me, father, thus to disobey
What thou commandest; but, I must maintain

The rights of my own manhood: when a child,
And until now, I have contentedly
Yielded obedience to thy every wish;
And held my duty, as a sacred right,
To be performed with meek alacrity.
No will of mine, however much desired,
Has ever reared rebellion's banner up,
Or raised itself antagonist to thee.
Thy every word has been unquestioned law,
A mandate whence there follows no appeal.
Thus far I have fulfilled the part required
From childhood's tender years; but what remains?
A *child*, I own, should e'er obedience give,
To each paternal law, without reserve:
But I have felt the springs of manhood rise
Within my quickening soul, awaking there
An independent will, a sense of power,
Of liberty, and life: and now I am
No longer what I was, a feeble child;
Dependent, helpless, only to be led
And guided by the strong parental rein
Of thy authority. I feel I am
A man, with conscious strength to rule myself,
And choose whate'er I will; and feeling this,

Cannot resign my rights, nor yet succumb
To mean indignities; which do belong
Only to slaves, and days for ever past.
I am of age, and therefore do entreat
That thou shouldst deal with me as I desire,
And give me now my portion of thy goods,
That, which to me does by my birth belong
Of thy inheritance and property.
Then I can make provision for my tour
As does become my high position, and
My noble rank.   For I would not desire,
By small appearance, or, by straightened means,
To bring disgrace upon our ancient house;
One of the first in this our glorious tribe
Of Judah; which tribe, upon the heaven-writ scroll
Of Israel's honoured names, does foremost stand.
Besides, I mean to multiply my store,
And by judicious means increase the stock
Of capital I own.   'Tis not my will
To squander, or, to waste what I possess;
But to return to this my native land
A richer, wiser man ; and better fit,
By large experience of these modern days,
To occupy my sphere.

Haden.

                          Misguided boy!
Thy warm impetuous spirit far outruns
Thy sober judgment: and thy passion casts
Across thy mental eyes so black a veil,
That thou canst not discern to what extent
Thy reason wanders. And thou dost forget,
All forms of duty, and all points of law.
Indeed, thy wild request is so unjust;
So full of folly, arrogance, and sin,
That I may well begin to question if
My son is sane. Does not thy knowledge tell,
That while my God shall spare this brittle life,
And lengthen out its short and feeble span,
What He has given, I hold in trust for Him
By my own right? That lands and gold are mine,
To use, or to dispose, as to me seems
Wisest or best? And dost thou then presume,
To ask of me, in form and language thus
Approaching to demand, for what thou hast
No right but in my grace? It would, methinks,
Be soon enough to cry, "Divide the spoil,"
When the possessor falls. Ungrateful son!
Is this a meet reward for those who've shewn

Unceasing love to thee, and ever sought
Thy welfare, and thy peace? But I will spare
Reproaches on thy head, for now I see,
'Twere better thus to be, e'en as thou wilt:
And thou shalt have all that thy soul desires,
As soon as legal forms prepare the deed
For its conveyance: then, thy portion had,
From out these wide estates, there is removed
All fear of quarrel and contention, when
I leave the scene. For, having had thy part,
What does remain, will by unquestioned right
Thy brother's be, his sole inheritance.
So thou shalt go, since all I have advanced
Availeth not, to move thy purpose from
This sinful way of disobedience.
A most revolting sin, whene'er a son
Plays the aggressor's part. To disobey,
Is numbered with the class of vilest crimes;
And yet there is another viler still,
Ingratitude! when love and kindness meet
Not only thanklessness, indifference,
And scorn; but foul contempt. Unjust reward!
These, Hamel, are thy sins; and though I pray,
That the Almighty arm of God's great power

May ever shield and guard thy wanderings,
Yet do I fear, and tremble while I fear,
That it will fall in judgment on thy head;
Armed with the rod of fearful chastening.
Or, it will leave thee, following unconstrained,
The deathly promptings of a heart depraved,
And held in Satan's power: that demon fiend,
Who in thy soul already hath begun
His hellish work; and will proceed therewith,
Till he has brought thy body, spirit, mind,
To yield to him, complete subjection.
Could'st thou behold, as I can see the doom,
Impending o'er thy head, thou would'st, methinks,
Pause on the threshold of the gaping gulf,
To meditate thy fate. But thou art blind
To every duty, and to all the forms
Of danger round thee spread; thy every step,
Each footfall in thy course, will waken up
A nest of adders, whose provoked recoil,
Will pierce thy inmost soul with agonies
Unbearable. And yet, thou wilt not take
My best advice; which would from this preserve
Thy wandering feet, and guide to brighter paths,
Where life's sweet flowers, profuse and fragrant grow,

All for thy happiness.   But thou art free!
A father's duty I have now fulfilled,
And more than that, my purpose is to give
What thou hast sought; I will on thee bestow
That portion of my goods which at my death
Would fall by right to thee: my living I
Will now divide, and give thy part in full;
With prayers and tears, that thou mayst use aright
This, and thy liberty.

Hamel.

    I thank thee, sire!
And yet thou art unjust to picture thus,
In colours so opaque, my future course.
But I will shew, by my consistent life,
How groundless and unfounded are thy fears,
And in how small degree I have deserved,
These sharp reproaches, and suspicious doubts.
If thou wast ever proud of me, thou shalt
Be prouder still, when I return again
From weary travel to my childhood's home.
Then shalt thou see my purpose was not vain,
Without design, or promise e'en of good.
My well-stored mind shall pour its treasures forth

Into thy listening ear; while from thy heart
Increasing love shall gush, to him who seems
Just now unworthy of its feeblest shew.

Haden.

AMEN, my boy! God grant it may be so.
But come, let us return into the house;
I feel the chill night air run through my frame,
Like some wild avalanche, sweeping to the plain,
From frozen glacier tops, where winter reigns
Eternally. Heaven's bright stars are out;
The clear celestial orbs of brilliant light
Adorn the vaulted sky, which does appear,
As with ten thousand diamonds richly set
Upon the garb of night. My star declines;
And thick-robed clouds begin to loom upon
The horizon of life. I thought my sun
Would sink in glorious light, to rise again,
By God's great mercy, in a brighter sphere.
So I presumed, but Heaven has not decreed
It should be so; what God decrees is best.
Then, why should I repine with murmuring speech,
When what He wills is for my good designed?
Help me, my God, to yield my life, my all,

A sacrifice to Thee. Let's haste within,
And tell as best we can, in careful speech,
Thy strange resolve, and my enforced consent.

The sun, which, in the cool of eventide,
Had sought its nightly couch, and sunk to rest,
Enwrapped in gorgeous fires, and pillowed round
With softly floating clouds of ether down,
Dyed in all-glorious shades,—was followed by
Pale Cynthia, in her pride, as slowly she
With graceful, queenly mien, rose in the heavens,
To occupy her lord's vacated throne,
And rule the night. And myriad stars came forth,
And cast themselves promiscuous round her way;
As courtiers fair, to pale their glory in
Her brighter beams, and run attendance round
Her brilliant course. And she had risen high
Upon the vaulted heaven, and had reviewed
Near half of her bright host, when Hamel came
Forth from the silent house, to gaze upon
The equal silent night: for nought did break
The solemn stillness, save the soft, subdued,
And timid sighing breeze; which sometimes bore

Upon its gentle wave, the distant howl
Of some nocturnal rambler o'er the dead,
From the dark vale that lay beneath him spread.
He gazed upon the soul-absorbing scene
With an indifferent eye, and saw not there
What others would have seen, the wisdom, power,
And glory of his God. He felt the winds
Play softly round his head, and gently fan
His wild excited brain to cooler mood;
But not a beauty of the midnight scene
Possessed one charm for him, or claimed a thought.
His eyes and ears, and all his senses were
Preoccupied with other weightier things;
Black thoughts of pride; that he had just obtained
A victory o'er his sire, and forced from him
Consent to all his plans; and thus he gave
Expression to his thoughts.

Hamel's Soliloquy.

Now I am free! Already in my soul
The wild excitement of this new-born life
Begins its potent work. Fool that I was,
So long to be content with childhood's dream,
The barren, empty form of craven life;

A misty nothingness, wherein the soul
Exists but with a name; for real life
Must ever strike its roots, deep in the soil,
Of free, uncumbered, independent will;
Else it's not life; but mean existence, which
Degrades the name. Such was my life,
But shall be such no more; henceforth, I'll live
In real earnestness, sip from each flower
Which in my pathway grows, the honied sweets
Of rich enchanting life. Yes; I am free !
And, Jehu-like, I'll drive impetuously
The sun of my bright destiny, amid
The envious, gazing throng of wond'ring men.
I've burst the bonds of semi-slavery
As Samson did his withs, and shake myself
Free from parental rule; that incubus,
Which as a night-mare press'd with crushing weight,
On all my energies. From hence I shall
Soar high above the trammelling forms of life,
And breath the pure elastic air of heaven
On strong, unfettered wing. Thus much has been
By perseverance gained; more than I hoped;
For scarce I thought to gain what I desired,
My portion now, in full acquittal of

All future claims. But I had studied well
My father's weakest points; which has secured
Such easy victory in this assay
And struggle for my rights. Thus far is good;
An omen fair of what the future holds
In its unmeasured store; a hopeful start,
In that untried career I have mapp'd out
For my terrestial course. My hopes are bright,
My means are ample, and my mind is firm
To make the most of what I shall possess,
To further my desires. For why should I
Deny myself of aught, when pleasures stand
Around my daily path with open arms
Of blissful invitation to embrace,
And taste their many charms? No, while I live
I'll live, and youth's best days to me shall bring
Their full supply of every earthly joy.
I'll pass no flower that holds sweet nectar in
Its petals fair. In every singing stream
That bears earth's pleasures on its silvery breast,
I'll bathe with rapt delight: and every ray,
From all the glorious things of this wide world
Shall centre in my soul their focus power.
My day has now begun, and its full orb

In bright meridian splendour shall proceed
Until it sinks to rise no more on earth.
Most fortunate of men! Oh, how I long
To spread my pinions, and away, away;
O'er hill and dale to fly, and like the dove
Which from the ark went forth, finding no rest;
But circling round and round from place to place;
Impatient ever, lest some unknown joy
Should else elude my grasp. Now I'll to rest,
And seek by blissful dreams to anticipate
What my bright star thus mirrors to my eyes.

SCENE II.

Interior of the Mansion. Morning. Haden and Hamel.

Haden.

Hamel, my son, I have desired that thou
Should'st meet me here, at this the early dawn
Of opening day, that, undisturbed, I might
Commune with thee. This is a holy hour!
As o'er yon distant hills grey waves of light
Come pouring on the scene. And carroling songs

From many vocal throats ring through the air.
And lowing beasts and bleating flocks unite,
With buzzing insects and harmonious winds,
To offer praise upon the earth's wide sphere,
In solemn, grateful anthems to the throne
Of Great Beneficence. Who can but feel
His presence at such time of general worship?
When all the busy throng of human life
Behind the scene lies hid; and God alone
In all His works is seen? I trust that thou
Hast sought His guidance, and His blessing, ere
From thy chamber thou didst venture forth,
To enter on the duties of the day?
Some fourteen days have run their circling course
Since last I held — midst yonder scented shrubs —
Communion with thee on a theme that mars
My life's supreme delight, and spreads a mist
Upon the polished face of all my joys.
Then didst thou ask, that I should give to thee
Thy portion of my goods in current coin:
A present largess, for thy sole control,
And to dispose as suits thine own desires.
Now I will ask, if thou art still unchanged?
And still resolved to tread this evil course,

Which surely marks the downward road to shame,
The end whereof is ruin and disgrace?
Or, tell me, son, if, in the narrow lapse
Of intervening days, thou hast reviewed
What I before have said, and in the scales
Of unwarped judgment weighed opposing claims?
And has the process wrought conviction in
Thy blind misguided soul, of erring thought,
And childlike foolishness? Has it restored
A sense of duty, love, and gratitude?
If so, thy father's heart will now rejoice
To hide in dark oblivion what has pass'd,
And take thee back within its fond embrace,
To dwell for ever there.

Hamel.
                    Then, hear me, sire!
I am accused of every form of sin
And lack of good; but this thou shalt not add,
Of indecision, or of fickle ways.
I am resolved, and more than e'er resolved,
To follow out my plans: for time has lent
Increasing strength to will, and made me feel
Impatient to be gone. I only wait

Thy pleasure, which to me seems long delayed,
Beyond the needful time the case required.
Yet, my chafed spirit would not openly
Rebel against thy will; still, I do feel
As does the wild war steed, when forced to yield
To tightened bit and reins; which, as he neighs,
And with impatient hoof strikes violently
The earth, yields to the curb reluctantly.
So have I felt at being thus detained,
When my whole soul is eager to be gone.

Haden.

My God is witness that I now have done
My utmost duty; I have warn'd, reproved,
Exhorted, and advised, all for thy good.
Now take thy lot; there is thy full desire;
Thy part in full of all I do possess.
I have surveyed my lands, estates, and goods,
And casting up accounts have meted out,
With just and equal hand, one lot for thee;
'Tis this I now present in full discharge
Of all thy future claims. Henceforth thou hast
No hope or expectation from the part

Remaining in my hands; which must descend
Intact and undiminished to my son,
Iddo, thy elder brother, who is still content
To dwell beneath my roof. And thou must sign,
In presence of our friends, this legal deed
And document, by which thou wilt declare
Thy claims all satisfied, thy portion had.
Renouncing thus all title, claim, or right,
To share again. And now farewell, my son!
I wish I could give thee my blessing; but
That must not be: my prayers, however,
Thou mayest always claim; and for thy weal
They shall unceasing rise, that God may give
A speedy light to thee; whereby the gloom
Of this perversity may all its foul
Enormity reveal. And may the God
Of thy forefathers go with thee, and guide
Thy steps from danger, and thy soul from harm.
And be to thee a sun, to illume thy way—
A shield, to guard in all thy wanderings—
A wall of fire,—a Rock,—a sure defence.

Hamel.

Farewell, my sire! Thy God will hear thy prayer,

And guide and guard me whereso'er I roam,
And bring me back in safety to my home.

Scene III.

Early morning. A Caravan in the distance. Procession of Camels, Horses, and Attendants, headed by Hamel. Haden on the Housetop.

Haden's Soliloquy.

And art thou gone! thou, whom my soul has loved
And doated on. Who hast entwined thyself
Around my inmost life, and deeply shot
Thy roots within the soil, engrafting thus
Thy being with my own, and making it
Almost essential to my very self.
How hast thou torn, with rude and thoughtless hand,
Thyself from hence? With lacerations deep,
Rinding the parent stem that nourished thee
With ever watchful care. God pardon thee!
May mercy overtake thy hasty steps,
And swifter still than thou, precede thy way;
For I behold how eager thou dost fly

THE PRODIGAL.   41

The home of those who ever held thee dear;
Thy father's home, the spot that gave thee birth.
How swiftly doth thy steed propel thee on
To unknown dangers, and to stranger friends;
Who by false ways, and empty, heartless love,
Will feed themselves upon thy ample means,
And suck the very life-blood from thy veins,
Till thou art left like a picked carcass, with
But skeleton remains.   To me thou art
As one already dead, for ever lost ;
For I can ne'er expect again to see
Thy fast retreating form, which by degrees,
Has less, and less become, as I have gazed
And mused upon thee.   Now, I'll look no more !
The road which winds its snake-like course around
Yon bold promontory, has hid for e'er
The wanderer from my eyes.   The stone is roll'd
Upon his living tomb; and in the words
Of Israel's psalmist king, my heart sobs forth,
" He shall not come to me, but I shall go
In God's good time to him."   And now, henceforth,
As day by day rolls on, while God preserves
The flick'ring lamp of life, my task shall be
To mount this topmost turret of my house

And watch from hence the path which last he trod,
Still hoping in the mercy of my God
To see the boy return.   Did not the son
Of the lone widow of Sarepta live
A second life, in answer to the prayers
Elijah breathed?   And may not I then pray,
And hope, and still believe, that God may give
Perchance, my lost one back ?   Hold fast, my heart,
On this thy last resource, and trust in God.

PART II.—Scene I.

Memphis in Egypt.

Thou Memphis! who
Upon the sacred banks of heaven-drawn Nile
Dost rear majestic thy time-honoured head.
Who in the earth wast mighty e'er the names
Of cities now renowned had from the womb
Of ever pregnant Time leapt into birth.
Whose shepherd kings had ruled upon thy throne
Long ere the conquerors famed in classic lore
Were known to men. And whose records do boast
A longer line of monarchs than belongs,
To modern empires of this bab'ling earth.
Light of the nations! Forth from thee there came
A radiating beam, to shine on all
The dark benighted corners of the globe,
And civilize its semi-barbarous sons.
Whose great ideas found embodiment
In towering works of art, of simple mould,
Yet grand in their simplicity. Within
Whose shadows rise, those silent, mighty tombs,
Of th' still mightier dead. And where is seen—

In temples grand, and gorgeous palaces;
In carvings, sculptures, and those rich designs
Which fill thy streets and decorate thy walls—
Thy ancient splendour, and thy present pride.
Wise in the arts, and deep in science read,
Yet, Oh, how ignorant of the things of God :
Thou know'st not Him who rules supreme above,
And orders all the destinies of earth.
How art thou fallen from thy father's faith
To marvellous depths of ignorance and sin.
Thy priests corrupt, thy doctrines all a lie;
Polluted are thy altars, and thy gods
Not worthy to be named: a countless host;
From the bright sun that rules in highest heaven,
To vilest reptiles of the lower earth.
In forms grotesque, and shapes abominable,
Thy deities are wrought; with human parts
To parts inhuman joined ; blending in one
The eagle, lion, horse; the ox and man;
With most unseemly shew of mystic sense;
Enslaving all thy sons in basest rites
Of foul idolatry. Corrupting too,
The neighbouring nations with thy impure stream
Of creature worship, and deology.

To thee the followers of the living God
Continually resort. In former times,
When thou was great and mighty in the earth,
To loan thy chariots, and thy mailéd men;
To help against Chaldea's swarming hosts,
And proud Assyria's conquering policy.
Till thou did'st falsely play the aggressor's part,
And in thy turn their conqueror became,
And led them captive to thy heathen home.
But Commerce now, has quenched the fiery rage
Of Demon war; and spread its influence wide,
Attracting to thy walls men of all tribes ;
The Greek and Jew; the Roman, and the Son
Of central Africa; that swarthy race,
Who bring thee tusks of ivory, and gold,
To swell the means of thy voluptuousness.
And there the Jew holds no inferior place ;
Within the precincts of thy ancient walls,
He is no stranger: multitudes reside
As constant dwellers, naturalized with thee
To live and die: with scarce a faint desire
E'er to behold their father's city, or,
Their nation's shrine again. And still they come,
The young, the profligate, and gay; to join

The saturnalia of unholy sports
Peculiarly thine own.   Unenvied fame !
A great absorbing cesspool for the land
That worships the true God.   What marvel then,
That all thy former glory's waning fast;
Or, that the Roman Eagle towers above
Thy Pyramids, and Sphynx ?   And his proud hosts,
Do domineer within thy sculptured halls,
Extorting from thee tribute for thy life.

In thy gay courts, young Hamel dreams he's found
A life of pleasure suited to his tastes,
And sensual delights; a constant round,
Of giddy whirling joy, that drags within
Its gold-edged vortex, those who yield themselves
To its alluring floods.   A vasty gulf,
Made pleasant to the eye, with flowery banks ;
Where fairy Nymphs join hands in gambols wild,
To Syren music, and display their charms,
With base immodesty : attracting there,
The unsuspicious youth, who rushing on,
Joins in the dizzy whirl, till down, and down,
And lower still he goes; then takes a leap,
And is for ever lost.   Mad pleasure this !

When noble heaven-born man, whose soul is formed,
And capable to feel the purest joy,—
Such joys as angels know,—can condescend,
To dash with headlong haste, excited lust,
And uncontrolled desire, to pass beyond
The line that marks him from the lowest brute.
Can that be pleasure, which arouses up
The deepest passions of the human mind,
And sends them forth as wild ungoverned steeds
Without a bit or rein? That wraps around
The pliant, loving heart, a steely crust
Of icy selfishness? That turns to gall,
The sweetest morsels in the feast of life?
And makes e'en life a farce, by robbing it
Of all its purpose, and of half its course?
Give it another name, and call it hence,
By its unfailing fruits, folly and pain,
Sorrow and bitter death. Thus should it be,
By all its votaries known, and to the world
Stand forth, in all its unmasked nakedness.
Arise, O Memphis! purge thyself from these
Thy foul impurities; else will the rod
Of fearful chastening fall, in crushing doom,
On what remains of thee.

Scene II.

A promenade in the environs of Memphis. Morning.
Hamel, Trophanes, Manchea, and others.

Hamel.

It gives me joy, my faithful gen'rous friends,
That I have been so fortunate to find,
Such kindred souls; else in your city, had
I passed my time in dreary loneliness ;
That, not the object whence I travelled here.
I shall upon your kindness then presume,
And now, at once enlist your proffer'd aid.
I am a stranger, lately here arrived
From distant Palestine ; from near the mount
On whose exalted brow, Jerusalem is built.
Your nation's wonders, and your ancient fame,
Have made me hither seek, to gratify
A taste for all that's beautiful and great.
And you shall be my guides in this desire;
Direct my steps, explain the secret things,
Writ in such strange, but meaning characters,
Upon your public monumental works.
And give to me the key, by which I may
Unlock their mysteries in my leisure hours,

And comprehend your figured alphabet.
Tell me the history of your nation's rise,
Explain its wonders, and exhibit them
To my bewildered eyes. Those pleasures, too,
For which thou art renowned; guide to their halls,
Throw wide their portals back, and lead me in,
That I may see and taste their magic sweets;
So will you yield such service unto me
As shall command abiding gratitude.

Trophanes.

We are thy servants; thou hast but to speak,
And we, as willing slaves, devote ourselves,
To meet thy full desires. But first receive,
A hearty welcome to our joyous land,
And strive to feel as if thou wert at home,
And rambling through the streets of Soloma;
Or o'er the verdant Mount of Olivet;
Or on the banks of Jordan, which descends
From Lebanon's tall hills and cedar groves.
And we will be to thee as kindred friends,
Dearer than all whom thou hast left behind
To mourn thy loss in fair Judæa's land.
Count on us, then; nor feel thyself as strange,

Or trespassing upon our utmost means
Of time or funds; a common property,
Kept for the gen'ral good, and from whose stores
Each fellow draws at need. Cast in thy lot,
So shall thy portion be made doubly rich.

Manchea.

Thou hast consulted well thy purposed plans
To visit here. For dost thou seek to know
The history of the past, when scarcely yet
The world had reared itself above the weight
Of deep o'erwhelming floods, and launched anew
Upon the surging waves of human progress;
To found new empires, states, and dynasties?
Here shalt thou find such relics of the time,
In ancient monuments, whose living tongues
Confirm each marvellous tradition; that,
Thou wilt imagine thou hast travelled back
To that dark period, when the gods came down,
And dwelt awhile in flesh with mortal man;
And whose immortal souls transmitted are,
Through all the various forms created life,
Has since their death assumed. Start not at this:
We know your nation claims to worship One,

A sole and only God, who will not give
His glory unto others, though they be
The highest in His realms, nor even share
With them His regal throne; who is removed
Beyond the utmost thought of feeble men,
Or even god-like minds. And strange legends,
Concerning this same God, are yet preserved
In our antiquities; of wond'rous deeds
Wrought in our capitol, and midst the floods
Of yonder inland sea, on your behalf;
When Egypt's pride and Pharoah's hosts were slain.
But this is written in your book of faith,
Of laws, and history; which also tells,
How, in the ages far from hence remote,
The sons of God beheld with loving eyes
The virgins fair of weak and sinful men;
And stooped from their high pinnacle to take
These maids of earth to their divine embrace;
From whence there sprang a race of giants, who,
Did rule the earth, and whose transmitted souls,
Their potency retain. And thus you see,
Our faith is almost one, proceeding from
One ancient common source, and merely turned
Into some diverse streams of human thought.

Chorus of Friends.

We all confirm what these our friends have said,
And offer thee our utmost aid to find
All that thou seekest here. And we will lead
Unto the very fount whence pleasure flows :
Those secret chambers where she constant holds
Her great levee in unveiled beauty, on
Her gorgeous wrought and e'er besiegèd throne;
The gushing spring of earth's sublimest joys.
There shalt thou drink, and satiate thy soul
With every good, till not the smallest want,
Or fancy of thy mind is unpossessed.
We know the goddess, and we are acquaint
With all the diff'rent forms she does assume
To lead her votaries on, and satisfy
Each aspiration for her smile benign.
No flow'ry path in which she deigns to tread;
No mystic thing her magic wand has touched,
Is hidden from our gaze. We worship her!
And in return she gives the choicest good,
Her kingdom can bestow ; more valued far
Than gold or silver, or most precious stones.
Then follow us, a happy, jovial band,

Intent on life; culling with careful hands
The sweetest buds, earth's only true delights;
And casting far behind each nauseous flower
That palls upon the taste; and like a swarm
Of cheerful busy bees in sunny light,
Sipping the nectar drop from every plant
That spreads aroma on the balmy air.

Hamel.

Thanks, thanks, my friends; your kindness unto one
So lately introduced, affects me much:
And I will show by confidence and love,
It has not been unworthily bestowed.
Already I begin to feel at home,
And venture now to ask your company—
With others you may choose—to sup with me,
To-morrow at my house. Then, when the sun
Has cast his fiery rays direct across
The banks of yonder Nile, and the dull tops
Of th' desert giants throw athwart the plain
Their dark unmeasured frown, shall I expect
Each one to bring his friend unto my feast,
That there we may confirm our new-made troth,

And pledge eternal friendship, peace, and love.
Till then, farewell.

   Friends.

      A seeming long farewell.

    Scene III.

 Interior of the City of Memphis. Hamel standing on his Housetop. Changes to the Interior of the Palace. A Feast. Hamel and Friends. Evening.

Within the heart of Egypt's ancient pride,
Her capitol! young Hamel had secured
A temporary abode. The outer walls
Looked dead and heavy on the narrow streets,
Without pretence of grandeur or display;
Except, were o'er the tap'ring portal rose
A carvèd image of the sacred bull,
Apis, the god of Memphis, to whose praise,
Egyptian genius had dedicated
Its gorgeous temples and its festal days.
Besides, there ran around the cumb'rous pile,
A belted band of subjects wrought in stone,

And representing battles, games, and shows,
With life-like force and speaking attitude.
Within the porch a paradise appeared—
Shut up secure from gaze of vulgar eyes—
Of spurting fountains, tall and graceful trees,
And green alcoves, which, formed of fragrant shrubs,
Spread a delicious perfume on the air,
Inviting by their quiet, cool retreats,
The wand'ring footsteps of each visitor.
It was a palace fit for princely guests;
And noble dwellers oft had filled its halls
With all the pomp of pride and vanity.
Those halls, supported on the massy props
Of graceful pillars, crowned with capitols;
And floors with marble paved, and walls that shone
With gems of native art, in tapestry,
And stone, and paintings rare; and round whose sides,
Were soft settees of most luxuriant make
And tempting touch; while fountains upward threw
Their cooling streams, diffusing freshness round,
And adding beauty to the magic charm
Which filled the place, and stamped its impress on
Each feature there. A promenade ran round
The upper floor, reached by a spiral flight

Of stairs and balustrades, guarded below
By wingèd lions placed on either side;
While on the top, two grinning monsters sat,
Of foul abortion; with hideous mouths,
Extended very wide, as if to gulp
Creation down; and rows of pointed teeth
That seemed to gloat for blood; and swollen eyes,
Which, in their fierceness, almost burst from out
The sockets, which confined them prisoners.
Just such a head was fix'd incongruously,
Upon a scaly, crouching, human form;
Whose toes and fingers represented were,
By curvèd eagle's claws; and from whose sides,
The spreading wings of that same monarch bird,
Were raised as if for flight. A garden here,
Of artificial mould, was tasteful spread
Upon the housetop, fill'd with all the charms
Of this and foreign lands, in choicest flowers,
Rare shrubs, and precious plants, which were re-
    nowned
For beauty, grace, or smell. And interspersed,
Were works in marble, statues of their gods,
Their kings, and senators. Hamel is there!
And leaning on the parapet's broad top,

His eyes are fix'd on where the murky Nile
Runs sluggishly along; and far beyond,
O'er th' hot sands of the distant wilderness,
To Judæa and his home.   Yet no remorse
Preoccupies his mind, for faults unseen,
And errors scarcely felt.   He glories now
In new-found liberty, as would a child
Delighted with the prize of some new toy,
Forsake all other things, and hope to find
In that one plaything all its heart's desire.
So now he casts all other thoughts aside,
And dwells on this as life's supreme delight:
Hoping therein to realise in full,
All he has promised to his sensual soul;
Without reproof, constraint, or childish fear
Of what might thence result.   With gladness then
He saw from where he stood his friends approach,
As in small groups they came from diff'rent parts
Of that old city, which, in gathering gloom,
Began to wrap the folds of solemn night
Around its stately walls.   A signal this,
For Hamel to descend and greet his guests,
With profuse speech of welcome and of love.
Then with a bounding heart, despising care,

And step as light as a young antelope,
He sought the hall of entertainment, where
The revels of the night were to commence
With a prepared and sumptuous repast.
A fit beginning — so his wayward mind
Declared that this should be — to future good.
The first step in the scale by which he 'll mount
To earth's sublimest joys.   He reasons thus,
As in the dark he strays of moral night;
And o'er his eyes the thick'ning film encrusts
Of sinful blindness, which deludes him on
By swift and sure degrees, from stage to stage,
Of deeper dark'ning death.   Yet, hear him speak!

Hamel.

It is my turn to bid you welcome, friends,
To this my table; and I do rejoice
To meet you here in such auspicious mood.
Think me not tame, or that my heart is cold,
If I should fail to tell you all I feel.
My wish is that each one may happy be
In this brief hour of social intercourse.
Let no dull cares obtrude within the sphere
Of this our circl'ing line; and if a thought

Antagonist to joy should trespass o'er,
And drop its poison in the sparkling cup,
Arrest the traitor, and expel him hence;
That every moment of our meeting may
Be sacred kept, and dedicated to
The god of mirthfulness. Let him preside
O'er this our festal, bacchanalian feast.
Spare not of aught that makes the table groan
Beneath its dainty weight, but eat and drink,
And quaff the brimful cup to friendship's toast.
Let every heart beat high, as glad and free
As morning rays upon the bursting gloom
Of opening day; when on with joyous glee
From hill to hill they skip, o'er plain and sea,
O'er fell, and flood, and field. So let our mirth
Untrammelled rise beyond conventual life;
And every tongue give forth its gushing stream
Of inwrought feeling, like an aqueduct,
Whose channelled way bears floods of crystal life
To one grand reservoir. Thus let our souls,
O'ercharged with deepest joy, empty themselves
Into the general store, that so we may
Partake each other's bliss and swell our own.

Trophanes.

We have obeyed with pleasurable delight
Thy gen'rous wish, to meet thee here, as low
The god of day, Osiris, bows his head,
And bids his queenly bride assume the reins
Of heavenly government. We hail her beams!
And from her throne invite benignant smiles
Upon our festival; but more than all,
The richest she can give from her full store
Upon the noble head of our kind host.
May all the gods — in all the various shapes
They have assumed, since by the giants they
Were forced to fly and hide themselves within
All forms of flesh, — unite to bless thee now;
And ever thwart the foul malicious schemes
Of Typhon for thy ill. And may the charms
Of all the amorous loves spread round thy path
A fragrant carpet of delicious sweets,
That every step may crush fresh incense from
Some fragrant flower just cull'd from paradise.
So shall thy days be bright, and each gay hour
Bear on its passing wing some new delight.

Manchea.

The gods can surely give no greater good
Than this we now possess.   True friends combined,
With heart and soul intent to stay the wheels
Of that old tyrant, Time ! Whose sharpened scythes,
Revolving swiftly round, destruction spread
O'er all their onward desolating course.
And if we must in some enfeebled hour
Yield to the gen'ral doom; yet, while we can,
No moment shall be lost to shorten more
Our brief existence.   But, with eager haste
We'll crowd our pleasures in, each treading close
Upon the passing skirt, and filling up
With body, life, and soul, the shadow of
Its predecessor.   Thus we'll add to life,
By ever living fast, and keeping pace
With our great enemy; whom, if we fail
Entirely to arrest, yet shall secure
Ourselves from falling 'neath his crushing car.
Life is the time for man to feast his soul,
And drink elixir from those silvery streams,
That flow so softly round his brief abode.
The fool alone despises present good,
For some unseen, but fancied future joy,

Which may elude his superstitious grasp,
And leave a shadow for his purchased pains.
We'll hold the present, make our heaven now,
And leave the future to its own account.

Mizraim.

My heart is swollen with such floods of joy
It must o'erflow, lest in the vain attempt
To stem its gladness, life itself should yield,
And pay the guerdon for such act of sin.
My soul ascends with those harmonious sounds,
That swell and fall upon the perfumed air
From yonder choir of minstrels, whose wise skill
Brings such sweet music from their instruments.
Just so our hearts are tuned, to one deep note
That regulates the rest, and holds them bound
Within its magic coil, a perfect chord
Of sympathetic love ; without a jar,
Or inharmonious string, to trespass in
With foul discordancy. Then let us sing,
And call the sacred Muse to aid our rhymes
With inspiration from the fount divine.
Let each one tell his tale of love's delight,
Of Syren pleasures gathered 'neath the stars

And treasured in the heart; and let him speak
In softly flowing verse; and every tongue
Join in a rapt'rous chorus to the song.
I will begin; the fire already burns,
And each shall follow in their sep'rate turns.

Mizraim's Song.

Come, come away from here;
  Away from city, temple, hall;
Follow me, companions dear;
  Hark! the voice of Dryads call,
    Inviting where,
    Unknown is care,
  And pleasures free as dewdrops fall:
      Follow, follow, follow, follow;
      Rural sports are free to all.

Come, come, the woodland glen
  Echoes now to sylvan strains;
Pan, with all his mongrel men,
  Keep their revels o'er the plains;
    They bound along,
    A gladsome throng,
  With whirling feet and giddy brains:
      Follow, follow, follow, follow;
      Fly from mortal griefs and pains.

Come, come, their mirth is high;
  To the sound of pipe they sing:
Hark! their shoutings pierce the sky,
  And make the starry concave ring:
    The gods above,
    Their joy approve,
And downward sweep on sacred wing;
      Follow, follow, follow, follow ;
      Gifts from heaven to earth they bring.

Come, come, they wait to share,
  All their joy with earthly mould;
Join the Fawns and Satyrs, where
  Joy is valued more than gold;
    Richest pleasure
    Without measure,
Satiates with bliss untold;
      Follow, follow, follow, follow;
      Silvery beams the path unfold.

Manchea.

Methinks our friend, Mizraim, oft hath been
A guest upon Parnassus' sacred heights,

And learned the secrets of the famèd Nine,
Whose temple there looks down upon the plains
Of neighbouring Greece. I cannot hope
To sing such flowing verse; for my dull soul,
Is but a stranger to poetic strains;
And not a spark will ever fly from thence,
Until the juice of Canaan's noted grape,
Has purged its fouler dross, and kindled up
Imagination's fire. But I'll assay
To do my humble part, lest I should seem
Unsociable and cold; or else appear
To cast a mantle o'er our festive mirth.

Manchea's Song.

Fill the bowl, the sparkling bowl;
   Lift the crimson cup on high;
Wine can cheer the drooping soul,
   And make the darkest shadows fly:
     Wine, wine, a health to wine!
   The vintage yields its precious blood,
   To drown our sorrows in the flood.

Pass the chalice round the board;
   Drink, and praise the god of wine;

Whose fountain is with plenty stored;
  Whose hands supply the draught divine:
    Drink, drink the vessel dry!
Old Bacchus rises from the Nile,
And owns our revels with his smile.

Every god, and goddess too,
  Twine their honours round his head;
Rich clusters in his pathway strew,
  While rivers flow at every tread:
    On, on, thou potent king!
Till with thy ruddy, laughing face,
Thou'rt known in every dwelling place.

Our friend Trophanes now must do his part,
To raise the mirth of each unfettered heart.

Trophanes.

I would not play the sluggard, when invoked
By such a just request to add my song.
Yet, where shall I begin, what subject choose,
On which to exercise my gen'rous muse?
For one has sung of pleasure with the gods;

Of earth's delights, in all their brightest garbs
And most benignant moods; while social joys,
Bathed in delicious wine, the burden was,
Of Manchea's latest song. Yet, while the world
With all its pleasure's good, and glist'ning wine,
To raise the sluggish brain is also good,
Still these are nought compared to beauty's charms,
And that sweet spell it throws around our souls.
To Beauty, then, I'll dedicate my verse,
And strive in song its magic to rehearse.

Trophanes' Song.

All hail to thee, Beauty! there's none can withstand,
   The charms thou dost everywhere spread ;
A net that entangles the heart and the hand,
   And enslaves from the sole to the head.
     Beauty, bright Beauty, thou queen of the earth,
     No heart can resist thee in sorrow or mirth.

The philosopher boasts of his stoical creed ;
   To despise thee he makes a pretence ;
But who, to his vauntings will ever give heed,
   That he's dead to the pleasures of sense ?
     Beauty, bright Beauty, thou queen of the earth,
     No heart can resist thee in sorrow or mirth.

The priest, too, will tell us thy smiles are a snare;
　All thy glory fast passing away;
And bid us of thy soft caresses beware,
　While his own feet are wand'ring astray.
　　Beauty, bright Beauty, thou queen of the earth,
　　No heart can resist thee in sorrow or mirth.

The soldier, the statesman, the peasant, and king,
　Each, regardless of state or degree;
To the shrine of thy temple their sacrifice bring,
　And own thee their chief deity.
　　Beauty, bright Beauty, thou queen of the earth,
　　No heart can resist thee in sorrow or mirth.

Then shall *we* annul thee, and set thee at nought,
　Whom the world hath agreed to adore?
We'll pledge thee in bumpers, and revel in thought,
　On the treasures thou keepest in store.
　　Beauty, bright Beauty, thou queen of the earth,
　　No heart can resist thee, or reckon thy worth.

Hamel.

My noble guests, how can my tongue express
The deep emotions of my grateful heart,

THE PRODIGAL.

For these united efforts to deprive
And rob existence of its lethargy?
I do already feel, while in the midst
Of such unselfish souls, more than at home.
My half-begotten fears of loneliness,
Have passed already from my sombre mind;
And to the womb of their abortive birth,
Have swift returned. Your friendship, too,
For one so little known, is doubly dear;
Unpurchased and unsought. What can I do,
To prove how much I prize this gen'rous gift?
Which to my need has come, more precious far
Than crystal streams to those, whose parchèd lips
Burn for the cooling draught, 'midst desert sands.
But small return is in my power to make,
For so much freely given; yet what I have
Shall at your service be; you may command
My time and purse, though poor the recompense
For such unselfishness. And now behold!
The Dawn of early day—unwelcome guest—
Breaks in abruptly with his slender staff
Of quiv'ring light, warning from hence
Each gladsome reveller. We must obey,
Though hard it is to bear a passing thought

Of separation, though for few short hours.
May Time, whose course has been since first we met,
So rapid for his age, now speed his flight,
And march more swiftly on, with giant strides,
Till we shall meet again. Till then, dear friends,
I bid you all farewell; and pray you may
Enjoy a sweet and undisturbed repose:
Let kind Imagination lend her aid,
To picture in your ever active souls
The image of the one he loves the most;
Or those delights which in your waking life,
Are most esteemed and rarest to obtain.

Chorus of Friends.

Farewell, farewell! yet know, ere we depart,
That thou, as yet, hast scarcely sipped the fount
Of pleasure's secret joys. Another time
We'll open out the scroll a longer turn,
And draw the dark'ning veil from such delights,
As thy unpractised eyes ne'er looked upon.
Then shalt thou find enough to gratify
Thy keen desires; and from the gentlest touch,
To realize such sweet exquisite joy,
As to confound the whirling, giddy brain.
With thanks, dear friend, again we say, *farewell.*

PART III.—Scene I.

A Panorama of the River Nile. A dearth in the Land of Egypt, caused by the scanty rise of the River. Hamel, in a state of destitution, from continued debauch, visits his professed Friends.

Far to the south of Afric's burning zone,
Where Abyssinian mountains lift their heads
In grand majestic altitude to heaven;
A tiny stream comes bubbling from the rock,
And sings sweet music down its rugged steep,
To cheer the plains below. And as it flows,
Receives with grateful mirth unnumbered rills,
Which cast their off 'rings to its treasury.
And thus increased, its limpid waters flow
Through Nubia's desert wastes, and parchèd sands.
Amidst the dreary solitudes of earth,
Which echo back the cheerful song of praise
It carols forth in nature's harmony.
With swift impetuous haste it then proceeds,—
As does the war-steed dash upon the steel,
In face of certain death,—till o'er the brink

Of Elephantine falls, it plunges down,
A mighty cataract! lost in a foam
Of crystal globes minute, and in its fall,
Dash'd into shivering atoms light as air.
Forth from the mass, resuscitate it comes,
And onward hies to greet the stately walls
Of old time-honour'd Thebes, and Thebian pride,
Majestic Karnack's halls! the glorious home
And palace of their gods. A wond'rous pile!
Glorious in ruin, stately in decay;
Where hist'ry fails, wrapt in the gathering mist
Of long-forgotten years. Ages remote
From modern chronicles, have borne to death,
Uncounted generations of the sons
Of this old Capitol. Here reigned in pomp,
A mighty race of potent warrior kings,—
Renownèd Pharaohs!—long ere Moses penn'd
The history of earth. An Osiritsen,
Thothmes, Ramasses; whose all-powerful names,
Have almost perished in the great decay.
Their tombs alone now publish what they were
Long centuries agone. Then they were great,
And stood upon the banks of that same Nile,
In all the pride of regal dignity:

Washed in its waters, worshipp'd at its shrine,
And dyed its rip'ling waves with human gore.
Where are they now? And what to them remains
Of all their glory? Just a few dry shreds
Of shrivelled parchment; formerly the skin,
Anointed, bathed, and clothed with sovereign care.
Unchanged the flood still rolls its tide along,
As blithe and free, and every whit as young,
As when the finger of creation's God
First scooped its channell'd way: unmindful e'er
Of empires, states, and thrones, which on its banks
Have risen, flourished, pass'd as dreams away.
Then past Dendera's ruins next it bends
Its sharp angular course; waking from thence
Stern mem'ries of the past: of priests and rites,
Of doctrines, tenets, creeds, material faith!
Whose clutching talons grasped created things
In all their various forms, and moulded them,
Into a system, built of subtle views
And dark imaginings.
Dendera! Famous for its sacred pile,
To Athor dedicated. Goddess of life
And all vitality. From whose ripe womb
Prolific, sprang the world on buoyant wings,

To float in ether clear. The sun and moon,
Bright stars and minor globes, creation all,
Was there ascribed to her, and worship paid
As universal queen. And on, still on,
The deep'ning river wends its serpent course,
Through all the fertile vale of this strange land
From south to utmost north; diffusing life,
Fertility, and wealth: and wandering e'er,
'Midst temples, halls, and tombs, and pyramids:
Old cities great and proud, and catacombs—
Homes for the living, and chambers of the dead.—
Undying works of art, whose polished stones,
Have braved the storms of time and ruthless man,
Since Cheops ruled, and Supis held control.
On this same river as the season comes,
The eyes of Egypt anxiously are turned
To watch its risings. Every inch is marked,
Each cubit noted down with thoughtful care,
As up the swelling flood creeps higher still,
Until the feeble walls that hold it bound,
Recede before its weight, and bow their heads
Beneath the gathering mass. Then on it flows,
O'er thirsty, parchèd fields, whose riven soil
Drinks in with greedy haste the welcome gift,

Long sought impatiently; till it becomes
Quite satiate with fatness, and repels
The fluid burden, with its weight oppressed.
Then it retires — its mission is fulfiled, —
And leaves the land refreshed, and belching full
Of its rich bounty. Next, the husbandman
Casts in the hopeful seeds, which, in their time,
Yield a full harvest for the people's needs.
Now, the whole land is glad, and each one brings
An offering to his god for gifts received;
And shouts of praise are heard, that good prevails,
And evil genii seek their desert caves.
But there are times when all their host of gods,
Cannot deliver from the haggard hand
Of tall, gaunt Famine; who, with monster strides,
Stalks o'er the helpless earth, which 'neath his tread
Recoils in abject fear. Just such a time
As Pharoah, in his dream, beheld approach,
When from the river there emergèd forth,
Well fed Hip'potami; and on its banks,
Feasted in verdant meads, till others came,
Half starved, and ravenous, and soon devoured
The sleek well-favoured kine. Then Typhon rules!
And gods, and men, and earth alike must bear

The brunt of his foul malice. Then the Nile,
Is held close prisoner in the narrow bounds
Of its own shallow bed, or scarcely spreads
Its needed draught beyond the muddy banks.
And here the heavens no recompense can give,
In fruitful showers, or earth-refreshing mists.
These are unknown, and all the nation's hopes,
Hang on the fickle and uncertain rise
Of that one source. Then does the hopeful seed
Lie withered in the earth, and hungry mouths
In vain cry out for food. The pasture fails!
And flocks and herds grow lean, on stubble fed,
Then famish e'en for that, and perish all
In one tremendous doom. O, what a cry
Of desolation, rends the burning vault
Of unpropitious heaven; whose brass-bound face
Reflecteth back the nakedness of earth,
And mocks its misery. When children cry
To men to give them food, and men reply,
With wolfish, vacant stare; when each one feels
Impelled, almost, to slay his dearest friend,
To satisfy his pinching, hungry want.
O misery of famine! A mighty one
Had burst upon the land of Egypt's swarthy sons,

THE PRODIGAL.

When Hamel found his means exhausted, and
His riches gone. His recent life had been
A downward course of profligacy and vice,
In which he had o'erstepped the lawful bounds
Of prudence, and of grace; and squandered all
His well-fill'd purse in rioting and shame.
Now he begins to feel the iron grasp
Of merc'less poverty; and looks about,
Some speedy way to find, how to recruit
His swiftly vanished store. No easy task,
Where all alike are poor; and none there are
So poor and destitute as those, who in their prime,
Have gathered round themselves, and called them
    Friends,
The gay, the vile, the profligate, and bad.
So Hamel found in his extremity,
When, by the force of outward circumstance,
Pressing demands, and vain desire to seem
All he had ever been, he was compelled
To use his wits to live. His jewels first—
Some heir-looms of his house, and prized as such,—
And ornaments were pledged, exchanged for shams,
To keep appearance up; soon all is gone,
Cash, jewels, precious stones, thrown in the lap

Of harlots and base friends. But much he has
From them as yet to learn, their love to prove.
To them with hope and confidence he flies,
Not doubting but, when once he speaks his want,
They will outvie each other with their gifts,
And gracious loans: so liberal in the past,
Has their unbounded promise ever been.
To Trophanes, as one on whom he had
Conferr'd more favours than on all besides,
He first departs, as certain of success
As that the sun had risen in the heavens,
And now pursued his clear, effulgent course.
To him he'd give the oft-desirèd chance,
To make full proof of friendship ever vowed.

Trophanes.

Most welcome Hamel! to my dreary home,
Made glad by thy bright presence. Tell me, now,
What wond'rous turn of fate hath brought thee forth
So early from thy bed. The hour of noon,
Has scarcely yet inscribed its narrow line
Upon the faithful dial. Our last debauch,
I fear has acted false upon thy tender frame

To hinder sleep. But, tell me, dearest friend,
How I can pleasure thee, and free my mind
From some small portion of its monster debt.
For, thank the gods, though there are those who say
The famine is severe, and rampant Death
Cuts capers o'er the land, we have not felt
As yet his icy touch. We have enough,
And need not then complain, or yield ourselves,
To sorrowing for the woes we cannot cure.

Hamel.

I am emboldened by thy *gen'rous words,*
To tell at once why I have early sought
A private interview. Our recent life
Has been, as thou dost know, of pleasure full;
One of unbounded revelry and mirth,
Which to sustain, my means were at the first
Both ample and to spare. But trifling helps
To my devoted friends, which to myself
Were favours also shewn, have lately been
So multiplied and large, that now I find
Myself to need their aid. I sought thee first,
Because I knew thy heart and bounteous hand

Were all benevolence; and might accuse
My little love to thee, if I had gone
My thirsty soul to slack at other springs,
Ere I had drunk at thine.

Trophanes.

What can I say?
I am distressed beyond the power of speech;
So feeble is the force of empty words,
They cannot half express my inmost grief,
The sorrow which in depth surpasses far
My poor expression. Had I the gold,
I would have now forestalled thy very words,
And doubled thy request ere it was breathed
Into my list'ning ear. A thousandfold
More glad to give thee aid, than to receive
The largest gift from thy superior love.
What can I do? My present case is such,
That I had thought this very day to ask
Again thy favour. Some, to whom I owe
Small debt of grace, but large advance of gold,
Are clamorous to have their payments made,
With bold ill-favoured speech, and threats of law.

Ungracious dogs ! thus to repay the debt
They owe to me, for patronage bestow'd.
Dear friend, accept this forced apology;
I would I could comply with thy request,
Which to my mind comes as a just demand,
Though urged by thee in soft and tender words.
O, that I could reply substantially,
With golden help; which to thy wants would add
More sure relief, than all my sympathy.

Hamel.

My trial is brief; a cloud that soon will fly
Before the sunshine which around me plays,
Of friendship's love. I do almost begin
To think it is a joy sometimes to feel
Dependent on our friends; that so we may,
Prove all the bliss of sympathetic love;
The depth and fervour of those kindly souls,
Which are by our prosperity obscured.
To Manchea, then, I'll turn my needy steps,
Make known my wants, and get them all supplied.
For he is rich; abundant is his store,
As I have often heard him boastful say.

G

A little, then, he will not greatly miss;
One bud from out his wilderness of flowers,
Whose perfume shall revive my fainting soul,
And make me rich, and yet not leave him poor.
Good bye, my friend! I hope when next we meet,
My purse will heavier be, and heart more light.

Trophanes' Soliloquy.

Good speed to thee, my dear untutored friend!
I scarcely thought thy blindness was so dark,
Or that thy heart resembled quite so much
The Papyrus' soft pith. Poor simple dupe!
How little dost thou know of all the wiles
Of this deceitful world, where every man
Lives for himself alone; and all the form,
Profession, boast, and talk of friendship is
An empty sham, a cloak that each one wears
To hide himself, and secret what he can
From others' filch. My aim has ever been
To cast my net where fishes most abound,
And not despise whatever comes to hand,
If I can make it for my purpose yield
One jot of good. Why should I net my game

For other men ? Or boast a false display
Of large beneficence, unnatural to man ?
If they have needs, let them reverse the odds,
And catch their own, instead of being caught.
My policy is this: are my friends rich ?
Then I to them am poor, and need the proofs
Of all their boasted love ; a liberal share
Of their superfluous goods. If they are poor,—
And few their numbers are that call me friend,—
Yet I am poorer still, in all but words,
Which are but little worth, and do not rob
The talents from my purse. 'Tis thus I steer
A gentle, even course, o'er every wave,
And fill my hive with various honied sweets
Cull'd from the life of many a blooming flower.

House of Manchea in the Suburbs of Memphis. Hamel enters.

Manchea.

Good cheer, sweet friend ! Of all acquaintances
That in our circle move, thou art the one

I most desired to see. A heavy curse,
Upon our nation lies, and famine stares
Each subject in the face. The very poor,
Have long been sending forth loud cries for bread;
But of the means quite destitute, have cried,—
Alas for them,—in vain. And slowly up
The foul disease proceeds, through all the grades
Of our afflicted state, leaving a track
Of pestilence and death. Thou know'st my wealth
Is all confined to lands, and their produce
My annual income yields, which for my wants
More than sufficient is, and margin leaves
To help my needy friends in their distress.
But this accursed Nile, whose turbid stream
Hath scarce six cubits ris'n above the mark
Of its accustomed course, presages ill;
And all my prospects blasts, which for the time
Proclaims me naked, destitute, and poor.
I know thy lib'ral soul will sympathize
With my misfortune, and such aid afford
As shall suffice for my extremity;
Until the gods beneficent prevail,
And golden harvests once more crown my fields.
Thus would I add debt upon debt to thee,

Which in due time shall all with interest full,
Be faithfully repaid.

Hamel.

Alas, my Friend!
How pleasured should I be to meet thy wish,
Could I but aught command. Nay, do not start!
Thou thoughtest that my store could never fail,
So large was the supply; yet, do not think
I would insult thy grief by pleading now,
What I but came to plead, my own foul needs.
My means are gone; and until Fortune's wheel
Shall make some lucky turn, I am reduced
To keen extremities. Yet, let not this
Protrude a severing wedge between our souls,
But closer knit, in sunshine as in clouds,
Our lives for ever one.
     (*Aside*) I know not where
I next shall bend my steps, for every hope
Seems equally forlorn; my friends all poor,
And those I thought most sure to prop me up,
Are most decayed and rotten at the core.
So much for show, a tinsel-gilded toy,

Which, in the glare of bright prosperity,
Assumes the dazzling properties of gold.
But let the damp, pestiferous breath of want
Pass o'er its polished face, then mark how soon
Its brilliancy is gone, and earth beholds
A black, abhorrent lie.
    (*Aloud*)
      Good bye, dear Friend.

Scene II.

Egyptian Country Scene. A Homestead surrounded by Fields and Pleasure Grounds, parched and barren, with Cattle and Swine feeding upon the scanty herbage. Hamel approaches with slow and timid steps, clad in the faded robes of recent grandeur.

Hamel's Soliloquy.

Lo! here I am, an outcast from the world
Of false, unfeeling hearts; plundered, despised,
Rejected, and unknown; while those who made
Most free to call me friend, are foremost now,

With cold, disdainful looks, to stand aloof
From my necessity. Fool that I was
To be so easy caught, and lend my ear
To such soft blandishments, and bow my soul
Before the hateful breath—so spicy then—
Of their time-serving praise. More foolish still,
To beggar thus myself, to gratify
The mean and sordid passions of my foes.
I thought them rich, unselfish, and the pith,
The very soul of honour; and if I
Should ever need their aid, it would not fail
To come as freely to supply my wants
As mine was giv'n to theirs. Vain thoughts, indeed!
Most credulous of fools ; to measure thus
Each man by my own rule : and now to reap
The black reward of my blind confidence.
O ! that I could from my keen mem'ry blot
This blearèd page of life's recording pen,
As freely as I now depart from where
My misery began. A retrospect,
That leaves dark shadows on the mind, and breeds
Doubts and mistrust of all humanity.
But mem'ry sharpens with the sense of wrong,
And closer cleaves around my naked soul,

Its last inheritance: and to my mind,
Torn on this constant rack, presents the ghosts
Of past extravagance. Empty I fly
From where I once was full; where guilty hands
Clutch their ill-gotten gains with eager grasp,
Or scatter it like dust, to meet the cry
Of their unruly, passion-governed souls.
Dark, perjured souls, stain'd with a thousand crimes,
That vainly cry for justice from the earth.
Vultures they are, with forms of heavenly mould,
Whose merc'less talons have sunk deep within
My trusting heart, and upward drawn from thence,
The very life blood of my every joy.
Yet why complain? My pride impelled me on,
And Passion's fire burnt fiercely in my breast,
Consuming there all reasonable control.
With hellish speed I ran the downward road,
That broad highway, which, by the busy hand
Of Folly's paved, with bones of victims slain;
But overcast by Pleasure's syren wand,
With lovely, fragrant, odorif'rous flowers.
This was the path by false ones pointed out,
As leading straightway to the gates of heaven;
Which following on, I scarcely here have stopp'd

Short of the mouth of hell. O treach'rous path!
Whose starting point is Beulah's pleasant land,
All bright and fair. But darkening tunnels span
The onward route, increasing more in length,
In number more—and wrapt in blackness which
Is more than felt—till landed at the goal,
The termini of sin, we realise
Want, and disease, and misery, and death.
. . . . . . Where shall I fly?
These vain repinings o'er the hateful past,
These gloomy thoughts upon my present state,
Will not restore my lost inheritance,
Or satisfy my hungry, starving soul.
When our first parent fell, God cursed for him
The late prolific soil, and bade him earn
His bread with labour and with sweating toil.
So I must reap the same reward of sin,
And hence content myself to work for bread
In foulest drudgery. Yet how unused
These hands have ever been to such base ends.
Nurtured with gentle care from infancy
Till now, have not I been a fav'rite child
Of Fortune's fickle choice? While all her stores
Have been, with lavish hand, cast to my lot.

Avaunt! I fly from torturing memory.
I was—I am—but O, what shall I be?
To yonder house I'll turn my sluggish feet,
And offer there my services for bread.

Amaraph (an Egyptian Landowner).

What ho! bold beggar. Pray by whose consent,
Dost thou presume to trespass on my grounds,
With such effront'ry? Say, who gave thee leave
Thus to approach my door, and what design,
Hast thou in coming here? Speak out in truth.
Or, by the sacred name of Osiris,
Thou shalt repent this most untimely show
Of thy audacity. I see thou art
A stranger in the land, and dost belong—
For so thy features tell, unquestioned proof—
To that accursed race, who once did serve
As slaves to our forefathers, in the time
Of Egypt's first and mightiest Pharaoh kings.

Hamel.

Thou speakest truth. I am of Hebrew blood,

And noble birth. And scarcely have the months
Which mark the cycle of the passing year,
Run twice their annual round, since first I left
That pleasant, fertile land, as did beseem
The rank and station I then occupied.
But here arrived, by reckless ways, false friends,
And famine driv'n, I destitute remain;
A homeless, friendless, helpless wanderer.
Judge me not ill; but, if thou canst, I pray
Commiserate my fate. Stretch forth thy hand,
And save from Death's cold grasp my sinking life;
Which fast is ebbing in his keen embrace.
So will I service give, and be thy slave,
If thou wilt but consent to give me food
Sufficient for my need.

Amaraph.

I hate thy race;
And do suspect thy word wanting in truth.
Yet tell me, now, what thou canst do to move
My pity to thy aid. Say, can thy hands
Wield right the useful spade, and drive it deep
Into the yielding soil? or guide the plough

In a straight furrow o'er the harvest field?
Or till, or sow the land? or reap, or mow?
Not one of these? For what, then, art thou worth,
If these are all beyond thy feeble skill
And weak capacity? Said I not right,
That thou art but a vagabond at best?
And worse, perchance, if I but knew the truth.
How would'st thou, then, that I should find employ,
For one whose hands no form of work can do;
Whose strength is all decayed, and life run out,
In vile, polluted streams of profligacy;
And whose debasèd talents only can
Devise dark schemes of unrevealèd crime?
I do but waste my breath to parley thus:
Begone! nor ever show to me thy face again.

Hamel.

Yet hear me, sir. For, though thy words are sharp
As barbèd arrows in my bleeding heart;
Still, strange to say, I am transformed so much,
I have no pow'r, or even wish to make
Resentful answer to thy words unjust.
So great the change calamity has wrought

On my once proud, but now subdued soul:
So strong I feel the love of life to be,
Though clad in rags, and to the grave's dark jaws
Press'd close by misery; that I must plead
Again compassion, with the earnestness
Of one that pleads to live. Do not I see,
On yonder parchèd fields and barren slopes,
Both flocks and herds, of cattle, sheep, and swine?
And now a thought breaks through the searèd crust
Of my distressèd brain, that I might act
The part of herdsman to the rambling beasts;
Supply their wants, or guide their thoughtless feet,
To where the herbage still grows lank and green.
Tell me, good sir, if thou wilt now consent
To this my plan, and save a wretched life,
Ere famished, stricken by the hand of death,
My wants and works together meet their end?

Amaraph.

I will have pity, since thou pleadest hard,
And hast devised a means by which thou can'st
Deserve thy daily bread. Yet, hear me out:
If this lean famine should continue long,

Thy part of that will be but small indeed.
Now go within; and rev'rent bow thy head,
Beneath the portal, to my household god.
Then with the servants, at the lowest board,
Supply with modest appetite thy needs.
And, with the dawn of heaven's reviving day,
Go to the fields, in charge of all the swine.
Guard them from danger, keep in proper bounds,
And give them husks to eat. And answer thou,
With liberty and life, to me, thy lord,
For their safe custody. Now, knave, depart.
See, I have giv'n thee charge; beware that thou
Art faithful to the trust reposed in thee.

Scene III.

A barren Country Scene in the same Locality. Hamel seated amidst a Herd of Swine. Coming to himself—Soliloquises. Midday.

Hamel's Soliloquy.

Abandon'd wretch! Vilest of vile I am;

Debas'd, polluted, lost.   I loathe myself,
And hate my very flesh, so foul with crime.
My life appears a black spot on the disc
Of sunny time.   Impenetrably dark,
Absorbing not, nor yet reflecting back,
One ray of light.   Wherefore, with reckless speed
Have I thus plunged into this gloomy pit ?
And what reward is reaped for all my pains ?
Hunger and shame, and misery worse than death.
For even that for which I sold myself,
Is now withheld.   The meagre pittance of
My daily bread, and nature's just demands,
Unsatisfied remain; while torturing Want
Preys on my vitals, and with thirsty lips
Sucks at the fount of my impoverished life.
Worse than these filthy animals I am :
These beastly swine, whose grunt abominable,
Incessant dins my ear, have husks to eat ;
And from devouring care, such as I feel,
Of memory and fear, are far removed,
As hell from highest heav'n.   What, though their joy,
Is in the miry water of the Nile
To roll themselves; and their delights are vile;

Yet are their wants and comforts studied more,
By our unfeeling lord, than mine, who own
The form of Godhead and estate of man.
Fain would I be as I behold them now,
Could I become oblivious of the past;
And from my breast for ever tear away,
All fear and dread of what the future hides
Beneath its sombre veil. O, depth of guilt!
From where I stand it were an easy step,
A small decline, a little lower down,
To take my level with the swinish herd,
And herd with them; feed on their dainty food,
And in their awkward revellings unite,
With equal filthy joy.
      My God! How near
I am upon the verge of manhood's precipice.
Wherein am I superior to the beasts,
Of souls contemptible? I call to mind,
That solemn hist'ry in thy sacred Word
Of Bab'lon's mighty king, who in the pride
And greatness of his pow'r, did lift his thoughts
In bold defiant attitude to heaven;
Invoking thence, from Thy eternal throne,
A grand display of thy supremity.

Till he, who stood and called himself a god,
Was from his palace and the haunts of men
Cast out as vile; to feed on herbs and grass,
And with the beasts of earth to take his place,
Till he should know, that the Most High did rule,
As King of kings, and Sovereign Lord of lords.
I now begin, as from a dream to wake,
A hideous dream, filled with the spectres of
Unnumbered woes, which on my spirits press
With fearful agony, like as of late
In my disturbêd sleep, the dread night-mare
Has often tortured me. The scaly film,
Which o'er my inner eyes has slowly formed,
Crust upon crust of opaque, hardened sin,
Is loosening fast, and heaven's own light illumes
My long benighted soul. I now behold
Myself as what I am, and estimate
My best estate as vile; my present, worse
Than deepest thought can gauge. Till now I've been
Beside myself, as one of mind deranged,
Bereft of all fair Reason's mild control,
And headlong plunging down, from deep to deep,
Through darkness unexplored, and pangs untold.
Like a dead weight cast on the ocean's breast,

Which sinks and sinks, through vast unfathomed
 depths,
With still increasing speed, till it rebounds,
And by the force of impulse thus obtained,
Ascends again to light. Can I ascend?
Is there for me one ray of distant hope,
To guide my wandering footsteps to the goal,
Of long-neglected, long-forsaken peace?
Returning Reason bids me lift my eyes,
To where the day-star of my only hope
Already gilds the skies; a far-off light,
Between whose flickering rays and my dark soul,
A vast abyss of murky blackness lies.
With eager grasp I'll clutch the messenger
Of slow approaching day; a day I feel,
Of hope and joy for me, of peace restored,
And countless sins forgiven. Haste, haste, thou Sun;
Forth from thy chamber come, and burst the gates
Of darkness from their holds, with gladsome beams
Of wide diffusive joy; that in thy light,
My re-awakened soul may now go forth,
From this polluting, sin-oppressive place,
To Mercy's outstretched arms and loving smile.
I will return! why should I perish here,

When every servant in my father's house
Has bread to spare; and feed the hungry dogs
On dainty morsels I would gladly take?
"I will arise, and to my father go"
Without delay; too long already I
Have this deferr'd, and trifled with my sins.
Now I'm resolved that nothing shall prevail
To keep me longer back from my lost home,
And from the feet of him, whose oft abused
But ever tender love, still yearns for me.
No fear of dangers in the untrod way;
Or pressing want upon my journeying;
Or base considerations of my state
Of abject, vile, and naked misery,
Shall now avail to plead the cause of sin,
Or longer keep possession of my ear.
"I will arise, and to my Father go,
"And say to him, 'Father, I have sinnèd,
"And am not worthy to be call'd thy son;
"Make me a hirèd servant in thy house.'"
I will abase myself into the dust,
Acknowledge all my faults, and pardon seek,
With supplications, bitter cries, and tears:
If so I may from his just anger gain

Some small respite, and hear his voice proclaim
Forgiveness to th' now repentant Prodigal.
O happy thought! It brings foretasted bliss,
As does the gale from far-off spicy lands,
Come perfume-laden, fresh from fragrant groves.
I am resolved! and e'er to-morrow's sun
Has hailed the birth of new-begotten day,
I will escape from this base drudgery;
From this death-stricken, hungry, famished place;
This most accursed land idolatrous,
To fair Judæa's proud metropolis.

Scene IV.

Early dawn. Hamel comes forth from his Master's House, and runs toward the Desert, which is seen in the distance.

The morning breaks forth from the womb of night,
Like a recovered angel from the depths
Of black unfathomed hell; with silvery head

Upreared against the vault of azure skies,
And wings that drip with pearly dewdrops on
The thirsty plains. The first faint tremulous wave
Of flooding ocean light, had scarcely spread
Across the jetty gloom, when Hamel came
From out the sleeping-house, with stealthy tread—
Like a weird spectre from its gloomy grave,—
And cast a cautious glance on all around.
He is alone; now gathering up the folds
Of his torn robe, with only staff in hand,
He swiftly flies, favoured by darkness, which,
Is scarcely yet dispelled; casting anon,
A timid glance behind; fearing pursuit,
Ere he can reach the desert's solitude;
More welcome now in its vast loneliness,
Than verdant fields and haunts of busy men.
Still on, and on, with undiminished strength—
Which for the time comes to his present need
With superhuman force,—he fast retreats,
Until he seems a match for Arab steeds,
Or with success to hunt the desert bird,
Which swift as lightning skims the burning sands,
But now he fails; his weary, aching limbs,
Refuse to do the bidding of his will;

" The deep-blue solemn skies" in streams direct,
Pour down their molten fires upon his head.
He stands at bay, and lifts his eager eyes
To seek a shelter, and escape from death;
More dreadful here by thirst and scorching heat,
Than by starvation with the swiny herd.
Joy! Can it be? O yes; his bounding heart
Leaps with new life, as yonder now he sees
The green Oasis, with its welcome shade
Of spreading palms, and rich fruit-burden'd dates.
Now hope revives, and on his mind exerts
Such wondrous power, that his whole system feels
The potent touch of the new messenger;
And braces up his failing energies to make,
One final effort to attain the goal.
Onward he speeds, and near and nearer draws
To certain life, which, ere frail nature fails,
He safely gains, and grateful casts himself,
Gasping and faint, beside the limpid stream;
Whose cooling fountain rises at his feet,
And sings sweet music in his languid ear.
He falls and drinks with wild and dangerous haste,
The silvery draught, until the fevered brain—
Like a strong bow too nearly over-drawn—

Resumes again its proper tone and power.
His hunger next, with rich ripe fruit appeased,
By bounteous trees with liberal hand supplied,
His heart ascends in full acknowledgment
Of heaven's good providence, which, to the birds,
And hungry, prowling beasts, supplies their meat,
And ne'er neglects His needy children's wants.
Again he falls beneath the spreading shade
Of verdant boughs, and courts refreshing sleep,
Until the sun toward the west reclines;
And evening shades come softly o'er the earth;
And cooling breezes fan the parched air ;
And kiss the aching brow of him that sleeps
O'ercome with weariness. Then rising up,
He leaves his grassy couch with thankful heart,
And strength recruited to pursue his way.

. . . . . .

Thus, day by day he marches on the road,
With doubts and fears oppress'd, and struggling hard
With half relentings o'er his purposed plans.
Now pride, now shame, then sorrow, force their way,
In marshall'd phalanx, and with serried ranks ;
Alternate battling in his aching breast
For victory. But good resolves prevail;

And, as he nears his peaceful home again,
Gather fresh strength to hold the mastery.
And Faith revives, and hopeful confidence,
In that insulted love so long despised.
And Love and Duty, each resume their place
With tenfold vigour, as he contemplates
The Past and Present with remorseful gaze.
O how he hates himself and all his crimes,
And loathes his very life, a life of sin,
Against a father's love; rebellious sins,
Renouncing just control, and trampling on
Heaven's own authority. . . . . . .
. . . . And musing thus
Within his troubled soul, he scarcely knows
How great a change has o'er the landscape pass'd,
Which lies around him spread. Not, as of late,
A scene of wild sterility, but rich
In all the various forms of active life,
Which Nature takes in her benignest moods;
Where Heavens, and Earth, and Air combine to rear,
A glorious temple to their Maker's praise.
No longer on the hot and blistering sand,
His swollen feet in painful steps descend;
No longer does the grave's dead silence awe

His restless mind into solemnity;
Or the vast sameness of the desert plains
Fatigue his steadfast gaze. The line is passed;
The dreaded wilderness, now like a cloud
Wrapp'd up in murky folds of vapoury gloom,
Spreads its full length along the horizon,
Where earth and heaven imprint their mutual kiss
Behind the wanderer; scenes of the past,
Which in his waking mind, already take
The unsubstantial form, and shapeless mould,
Of some oppressive, terror-clothed dream.
He starts from out the long-nursed reverie,
As one awaking from a conscious sleep,
Surprised to hear the sounds of Nature's life:
The oxen lowing on the grassy slopes;
The shepherd's harp amidst his bleating flocks;
And noisy barkings of the faithful dog,
Aroused to watchfulness by distant howls
Of hungry, prowling wolves; and airy tribes,
Uniting their sweet notes in various songs
Of heaven-ascending praise; and thrifty bees,
Collecting precious stores from fragrant flowers,
Hum out their music in the listener's ear.
While Nature all, dressed as a bride adorned,

And breathing fragrance from ten thousand pores,
Invites attention from the Traveller,
And hails with gladsome joy his late return.

He pauses here: the weary, way-worn youth,
Halts in his journeying. Again he stands
On Palestina's soil, his native land;
Around whose sacred shrine fond memories cling,
Of happy childhood's days; when like a roe
On Carmel's height, or Lebanon's fair hill,
Joyous and free, he bounded gladly o'er
The emerald velvet plains; or blithely sang,
Without a shade of care or thought of sin,
His simple, infant lays. How changed he feels,
As thus his thoughts revert to what he was;
As in his soul the images arise
Of bygone days; each object, spread before
His vision's utmost stretch, is full inscribed
With well-known characters, engraven deep
Beyond the power of distance, or of time,
To mar, or to efface. Yet, 'midst them all,
His father's earnest love conspicuous shines,
As the fair moon—ruling the starry heights
Of heaven's deep firmament,—with silvery rays

Pales each inferior orb, and bold proclaims
Herself, amidst the royal globes of night,
A Queen of queens; just so that father's love,
Above each pleasing recollection stands,
Supreme and grand. His childhood's bulwark, and,
His manhood's pride.

PART IV.—Scene I.

Evening. The Mansion of Haden on the Mount of Olives. Haden standing upon the lofty turrets of the Watch-tower. Hamel approaching in the far distance.

Haden.

With wearied limbs and almost broken heart,
Again I reach this dizzy altitude,
Still hoping that my God will hear my prayer,
And give me back my son. Three times the months
Have run their circling course since last I saw
His fast retreating form. And every day,
As day by day has passed, of these slow years;
I have ascended to this hallowed place,
To plead with gracious heaven on his behalf,
And watch the issue of my burdened cry,
" How long, my God ! How long ?" And these
    dark years,
Have on my system wrought a life's full work,

And supp'd the fountain dry. My strength is gone,
My manhood's power decayed; the pitcher's broken,
And the silver cord is loosening fast.
Yet I do feel a strange sensation round
My slow pulsating heart; a sudden glow
Of life-reviving warmth; what can it be?
Dared I again to hope, I should believe
It were a sign, a token from on high,
My prayer was heard. Why should I tremble thus?
Tremble to hope; and fear my God to trust?
But I have hoped, and hoped against all hope,
Reaping but disappointment for my pains,
Until my heart is sick, and fainting now
With long-deferr'd desire. What can I do?
Each time I've risen as on eagle wings,
And boldly swept toward the open sun,
Each time I've failed, and fallen from the heights,—
To which my folly's insufficient strength,
Had borne me far,—to deeper, vasty depths.
Therefore I fear, even when thus I feel,—
As now I feel,—heaven's promptings in my soul.
I will obey, and once more scan the scene,
With eager searching eyes; a scene of peace,
All calm and radiant in the golden tints

Of yon declining sun. Just such an eve
As this lay on the earth, when first I heard
My boy's sad purpose to depart from home.
When in the grounds which at my feet lie spread,
I strove to move him from his sinful plans,
But strove, alas, in vain. Then I beheld,
As he directed me, those glorious towers,
Whose heaven-aspiring heads, on Zion's height,
Were clothed in purple floods of eventide,
As now they shine; and all the fruitful vines,
Hung low their burdened boughs of juicy grapes;
And yonder fields, waved their tall stems before
The gentle summer breeze, bowing their praise
To heaven's all-sovereign Lord.
       Be still, my heart!
Deceive thyself no more with groundless hopes,
Built up to be destroyed, born but to die;
And leaving nought but ruins, heap on heap,
To choke thy future joys. Yonder, afar,
A little speck I see, a tiny spot;
Yet why should this demand a thought from me?
I have ofttimes beheld the like before,
And yet have never felt so strangely moved.
It may be but a stray, neglected beast,

Seeking fresh herbage on luxuriant soil;
Or some poor wand'rer plodding far from home,
His toil-worn, anxious way. Again this heart,
Throbs with unwonted violence in my breast.
What can it mean ? It seems, as now I look,
Some potent charm were binding fast my soul,
To that far-off and undefinêd mark.
I still must gaze, as did Gehazi look
Upon the rising cloud; so small at first,
As to appear no larger than a hand;
Then spread itself, and covered all the land.
This way with steady course it onward comes,
Diverging nothing from the line direct.
As nearer now the dusky shape inclines,
I see it bears the God-like form of man,
But, as it were, bowed with a weight of years,
Or heavy misery. For now I see
His robe is humble, and his modest staff,
Betokens poverty. So our great sire,
The honoured Jacob, once a Pilgrim was,
As poor and sad as he.
     How my head reels !
What do my eyes behold ? O, can it be ?
It is! Be calm, my burning brain, be calm:

Come back, my truant senses, into life:
Desert me not in this extremity.
My God, my God, attend and hear my prayer.
Am I deceived ? Does not a father's eye
Detect the image of his favourite son,
The reflex of his own lost youthful prime,
Though hid in rags, and bowed with misery ?
It is my son ! My own beloved son !
The lost, and prayed for, Hamel, my dear son.
Haste, haste, my tottering limbs ; bear me to greet
With words of kindness, the repentant boy ;
Call back the fleetness of thy younger days,
Lest my full heart should with this sudden joy,
Burst out of life, ere I can grasp him in
My loved embrace.

Scene II.

Open Fields. Hamel slowly advancing, resting upon his Staff, and with his Eyes fixed on the ground. Haden rushes in, followed by Servants, and falls upon the neck of his Son.

Haden.

Hamel, my son ! My God has heard my prayer,

And spared my life to see thy safe return:
Kiss me, my son.

Hamel.

"My father, I have sinned:"
Against the laws of heaven I have rebell'd,
And thy mild sway. Thy just authority,
I've wilfully despised; and set at nought
Thy loving, gentle rule. I do repent:
Am sorry for my sins; and own with shame,
My base simplicity. For this I came,
That I might tell thee all my spirit feels,
And pour my sorrow's growings in thy ear;
And hear from thee,—if thou canst speak the word,—
A pardon for my crimes. I do confess,
"I am not worthy to be call'd thy son;"
And only seek forgiveness at thy hands,
For all my wilful ways: those sinful ways,
Which here I promise ever to renounce,
As God shall give me grace.

Haden.

My son! my son!

Hamel.

Call me not *son*; I have no claim thereto:
And must henceforth resign the very name.
I am content, if thou should'st judge me meet,
To be a servant . . . .

(*Haden, to a servant.*)

. . . . Adoni! run,
And fetch the choicest robe my house contains;
That one reservêd for the honoured guest
On festal days; and clothe my son therewith.
And bring the richest sandals thou can'st find;
Those finely carved ones, with silken cords
Entwined with threads of gold; anoint his feet,
Then lace the sandals on.—And put my ring,
My signet, on his hand; the pledge of love.
Then lift thy trumpet voice, and loud proclaim,
To all the world, "My son."
                              And thou, Aaron!
Haste to the oxen's stall, and loose from thence,
The youngest, fatted calf; then kill, and dress,
And for the festal board with speed prepare,

That we may eat, and in our hearts rejoice,
With merry gladsome joy, and thankful glee.
And thou, Kohath ! do thou direct the feast,
And make provision with thy utmost skill,
To swell our happiness. Go forth, and seek
Through all Jerusalem, for those who play
With clever hand upon the harp and viol:
For chief Musicians, who, with heavenly strains,
Shall lift our rapt'rous souls to ecstasy,
And full enjoyment of this happy day.
" For this, my son, was dead, and is alive ;"
" Was lost, and," lo, to us again, " is found."
Come now, my boy, no longer use thy staff,
But rest on me: I will conduct thee in
To this thy home again; thy welcome home,
Made glad by thy return ; as naked earth,
Revives before the joyful face of spring.

Hamel.

I am unworthy; yet, must needs comply
With this thy own request. Lead on, my Sire.

Scene III.

Interior of the Mansion. A large Hall filled with Guests and Dependants feasting and rejoicing. Musicians playing their Instruments.

Haden.

Hear me, my friends ! Give ear to Haden's speech:
The old man tottering on the verge of death.
" I have been young,"—as Israel's Psalmist said,—
" But now am old;" my head is silver'd o'er,
By Time's unsparing hand; thus stamping me,
Mortal for immortality.
And I recall the mercies of my life,
A countless host of blessings, which arise
To challenge now my praise. Yet, in them all,—
And many now stand forth conspicuously,—
There is not one to equal in delight,
This last, and crowning mercy of them all.
For this I tax the remnant of my strength,
To raise a song of loud, far-echoing praise;
A pealing note, which shall ascend to where
In the high heavens our Sovereign Maker reigns.
And you, my friends, make this a gladsome day;

Let rich exuberant joy fill every soul,
And unconstrained gush forth : drown every care
In thought of present good; and in that good
Disport yourselves, as freely as the tribes
Of the vast ocean in their buoyant sphere;
Or, golden-plumaged birds in ether-air.
Let every heart beat loud in unison
With each vibrating motion of my own;
And every soul send forth its separate stream,
To swell the tide of our unfathomed joy.
And you, my servants, next to my own sons,
The objects of my care;—in all your grades,
From Kohath, my good steward, who directs
The various business of my wide estate;
To humble Jacob, who, with faithful zeal,
Performs the menial duties of my house,—
Join all as one in this gay festival ;
And let your mirth rise high to celebrate
My son's return ; the dead restored to life.
Let one and all, friends, kindred, neighbours, each
Assembled in this hall, servants and slaves,
The young and aged, with the bond and free,
Make merry and be glad: join hearts and hands,
In cheerful, happy dance ; let every step,

Fall light and glad, as dew on parchêd grass,
To sound of music, and to voice of praise.

Then they began,—each one as suited best,—
To make all merry. The invited guests,
Sat round the spacious hall, on raisêd seats
Carved curiously; and covered with
Damascus cloth of gold; while o'er their heads,
And round on every side, in gay festoons,
And graceful, pendant folds, the curtains hung
Of this same precious cloth; with birds and trees,
In various strange designs inwrought thereon.
Before a table spread with dainty meats,
And viands rich,—of which the fatted calf
Holds the most honoured place,—they all recline;
While servants with good will pass to and fro,
To anticipate their wants. And the old man,
With eager, anxious eyes, from where he sits,
Sees all supplied. Then, with a hearty will,
And cheerful, loving speech, they eat and drink;
And pass the love-cup round the burdened board;
And pledge in moderate draughts of simple wine,
The health of Haden, and his new-found son.
And strains of music fill the vaulted roof,

And roll in soft vibrations round the room;
Hushing the soul of every listener,
To sweet harmonious cadence with itself:
Or calling up from the deep chamber'd vaults,
Of every human heart, its passion floods,
In surging waves of sensitive delights :
As wildly now it swells majestic forth,
And rides upon the perfume-laden air.
In quicker, livelier strains it next proceeds,
Now the repast is o'er; each seat is left,
And all are gathering on the central floor;
Where on the light and fairy tripping toe,
They dance with mirthful glee, to measured time,
And heart-tuned harmony: shouting their joy,—
Which as they bound and turn, then bound again,
With whirling feet, and giddy, swimming brain,—
Knows no control. . . . .
. . . . Midst this bright galaxy,
The clear ascendant star of Hamel shines;
So long obscured, that now its lustre shews
With more supreme effect ; dazzling the eyes
Of all those lesser spheres that round him play.
But chiefly one is drawn, by pity first,
For his late suffering in a distant land;

And then by admiration of himself.
With bashful eyes, and half-averted head;
With blushing cheek, and heart that palpitates
More freely than is wont; fair Esther owns
The secret to herself; and wraps the garb
Of maiden prudence round the subtle joy,
In many a tightening fold; lest by some word,
Or look, or motion, she should else betray,
The secret-workings of her inmost soul.
Yet not alone, is Esther in her love;
For Hamel's eyes have watched her at the feast,
With earnest, steadfast gaze; and many a scene,
Mix'd with their childhood's days, has he recalled,
With timid speech, and brightening hopes upraised,
To her approving, inattentive ear.
Of gambols by the Kidron's silver stream ;
And wild-flower seekings on the graceful slopes
Of Olivet's far-famed, and fruit productive hill;
Where they so freely talked of mutual love,
And laid their plans for future, unborn years.
Now in the merry dance he leads her forth,
His chosen partner ; watching her every look,
And on her words, hanging with fond delight,
And life inspirêd hope. Thus mutual joy

Fills their united souls; eye answers eye,
And thought with thought agrees; and childhood's
    dream,
Finds its awaking life, in manhood's love;
As heart reads heart, and soul to soul confest,
Throws off the garb of fortress-bound reserve,
And naked stands, each to the other known.
Oh envied pair! For who can tell the joy;—
Or measure out the sum of earthly bliss;—
The pure unselfishness;—the perfect peace;—
The placid depth of joy;—of youth's first love?
Is there a flower, from heaven's bright paradise,
That blooms on earth? Is there a bliss,
That rises far above all happiness?
A fragrance, whose perfume o'erpowers all scents?
This is that fragrance; this that perfect bliss;
And this that precious flower, from heaven sent down,
Ambassador to earth. Heaven prosper thee,
Young Hamel, in thy suit; and soon fulfil
Thine utmost heart's desire; that her thou lov'st,
May to thy manhood cling with fond embrace;
As does the ivy twine itself around
The stalwart oak.

Scene IV.

Iddo, the eldest Son of Haden, approaches from the Fields, and ascends the Slopes of Olivet, toward his Home.

Iddo, (soliloquizes.)

To scale the Mount of Olives is a task,
When one has laboured all the passing day
Out in the open field, tending the flocks,
And leading them to where the pastures green,
And spreading trees afford a grateful shade,
From noontide's sultry heat. But soon I hope
To rest my aching limbs, now wearied out
By three days' travel over hill and dale.
For thrice the sun,—which just now bowed his head
In majesty supreme beneath the folds
Of yonder burning clouds,—has risen and set,
Since I departed hence to ascertain,
The state and welfare of those distant herds
Of cattle, which belong to my good sire.
No doubt, the good old man is anxious now
For my return, and thinks I tarry long.

Ofttimes, when I before have thus deferred
My coming longer than I did intend,
His filial love has prompted him to come,
And meet me ere I reached his treasured home.
Most gladly then I 've seen his silvery locks,
Play in the gentle breeze, and heard his voice
Of welcome wafted down the hill's fair side;
Than which, no sweeter music to my ear,
Was ever borne. And much I wonder now,
That I to night have travelled thus so far,
Without these usual tokens from my home.
O can it be; my timid heart suggests,
My father's ill, or worse, perhaps is dead;
And I away, robb'd of his blessing, with
Departing breath. Haste on, my slothful feet;
My heart be still; perchance my fears outrun
The sober fact; and some slight accident,
A visitor, perhaps, has kept the old man in.
And now I see the house is all illumed;
From every window stream bright rays of light;
And forms are flitting to and fro therein,
With hasty step. Again my fears return;
What do I hear? The sounds of music, and
The tripping feet of those who dance thereto.

My puzzled brain tries, all in vain, to sound
The mystery. Lo ! Kohath comes; I'll shout,
And ask him, why the old ancestral house
Is of its wonted quiet thus despoiled,
By maddening revelry. Kohath, ho !

Kohath.

My master's son ! I heard thy voice with joy,
And ran to greet thee with most willing feet.
Thy coming here is timely,—for thy sire
Has watched, expectant, all this happy day,
For thy return; that thou shouldst also share
The great rejoicing.

Iddo.

What mean you, Kohath ? Wherefore all this show ?
For whom this music, and those merry shouts
Of laughter, song, and mirth ? My fancy's dreams,
Would almost make me think, my father had,
In his old age, begot another son,
As Abraham did of yore; and in his glee
Had thus forgotten all his sage control,

For joy thereat. But, why do I surmise?
Tell me, at once, for I desire to know—
What is the meaning of this wondrous change?

Kohath.

Hear me, kind Iddo; thou hast nearly guessed
The real cause of all this mirthfulness.
Thy father hath not found another son,
An infant from the womb, to fill his heart
With pride, and youthful love; but, better still,
A son long lost, and mourned as with the dead.
Thy brother, who, long since departed hence,
Is come again; and, for the joy thereof,
Thy father hath served up the fatted calf,
Because he hath received him safe and sound.
Then enter, Sir, and join the gladsome throng.

Iddo.

I am amazed at this intelligence!
Yet, not so much to hear the boy's returned,—
For, soon or later, that I did expect,—
As that my father should so easy yield

To his cupidity; and with ado,
Such as my ears surmise, have welcomed back
This base, ill-mannered scion of our house.
My anger burns indignant at the thought
Of folly so expressed; and all the chords
Of my attunêd soul, instinctive shrink
From contact with such foul discordancy.
Think not that I will countenance the sham
Of his humility; or lend my face
To vagaries such as these now passing here.
I'll stand aloof, and disregard the slight
Cast on myself, by one whom I have served
These many years. Provide me, Kohath, then,
A separate room; and bring refreshments in,
For much I need, both them, and also rest.

[*Ex. Kohath.*

Enter HADEN.

Haden.

What ho, my son ! Thou art thrice welcome here,
At this auspicious hour. I thought thee long
Upon the tedious way, and now come forth,

From out the festive scene, to look for thee.
Thy brother Hamel is returned again,
To his forsaken home, a better man;
And we are glad, and friends and kindred join
In kind congratulations, and in mirth,
To welcome the wanderer back. And thou,
As I have done, wilt now embrace the youth;
Who, mourning o'er his sins, and penitent
For all misdeeds, seeks to be reconciled.
Come, then, my son, join hands in fellowship
And frank forgivings for the buried past.

Iddo.

I have done much to please thee, honoured Sir,
And gladly would do more, could I but feel
That I therein preserved my dignity;
But never yet have I demeaned myself
To grovelling acts, or made the least pretence
To base hypocrisy. Forgive me, then,
If I in this refuse to do thy will.
And wherefore, may I ask, is all this mirth?
For *one* whose whole career is steeped in crime;
Whose very name is a reproach to us,

And whose return, methinks, should rather be
Announced in sackcloth, and in voice of woe.
Art thou beguiled to think him now sincere,
Without a further proof than his frail word?
Truly, my father, I had thought thy soul,
Quicker by far in just discernment.
And have not I, by this, thy partial love,
Good cause to marvel, and to take offence?
I wondered why I did not sooner meet
A greeting from thee, as is usual, when
My absence is deferred; that point is cleared,
Another hath more worthy filled my place.
" Lo, now! these many years I've servêd thee
" With a devoted love, neither have I
" At any time transgress'd thy lawful word;
" Yet, hast thou ever made for me a feast?
" Or given one tender lamb, that I therewith
" Might with my friends, make merry and be glad?
" But, lo! as soon as this thy son is come,
" Who hath with harlots eaten up thy goods,
" Devoured thy living, squandered all in sin,—
" Without delay, thou 'st kill'd the fatted calf;
" And all for him, whose name my very lips
" Do almost loathe to speak." Think me not harsh,

Unfeeling, or unkind, that I do thus
Express myself, because I feel that here
My cause is just; and thou, my father, art
But partial in thy ways.   Then urge me not,
But now return to *him*, and leave me here,
For I would be alone.

Haden.

       Hear me, Iddo !
Methinks thou dost not well to argue thus,
Seeing thou hast no cause but in thy fears;
And for the rest, 'tis pure imagining.
Art thou not ever with me in the house,
Sharing my honour, ruling through my love,
And ever doing what to thee seems best ?
And dost thou not most fully understand,
That Hamel hath already had his part
Of all my worldly goods, and cannot hope
Ever to share again?   If he is poor,
Still poor he must remain ; for thou art heir,
Sole heir, of all my lands; yea, more than that,
Of all I do possess:—all that I have
Is thine exclusively.   Then judge not ill,

But freely do forgive, as thou dost hope
Thy Gracious Maker shall to thee extend
Forgiveness for thy sins.   " It was but meet
" That we should merry be, and also glad;
" For this thy brother was to us as dead,
" And is alive again; was reckoned lost,
" But now again is found."   Come, then, my son.
                                    [*Ex. Haden and Iddo.*

Scene V.

A Chamber in the house of Haden. Haden sitting on his Bed. Enter Iddo, Hamel, Miriam, Esther, and Friends. Twilight.

Haden.

Draw near, my friends: for fast my strength declines,
And slowly through my veins the crimson tide
Now ebbs and flows.   The vital spark, also,
Of my existence, is but feebly kept
From passing into darkness, and the shades

Of cold and conquering Death. Yet, ere I leave
This land,—which God has given to us and ours,—
And all the fond, endearing ties of life,
For that blest state, of which this is the type,
And semblance faint,—I covet the desire,
Beyond all other things, to see my sons—
The pillars of my house, and whose embrace
Is now a pledge of their restored love,
And sweet accord, as brothers true in heart,—
United to the virgins whom they love,
By matrimonial vows. " For God beheld,"
When Adam first was made, " it was not good
" For man to be alone," and therefore gave
A helpmate unto him; a second self,
To share his sorrows, and increase his joys.

Come to me, Iddo. Thou, my first-born son,
I constitute my sole, legitimate heir.
Long hast thou loved, and been in turn beloved
By Miriam, thy fair cousin, who now stands
Blushing to hear her name pronounced with thine.
Take her, my son, and may God multiply
Thy living seed, as stars in heaven, or sands
Upon the wave-assaulted beach. And may

The pearly dew rest on thy pasturing meads;
And flocks and herds increase; and faithful friends,
Their numbers multiply; and all thy foes—
If foes should ever rise to cross thy path—
Bow down and lick the dust. And may the smile
Of an approving God be ever thine;
A sun to shine on thee, a shield to guard.
And may thy sons pronounce thy name as blest,
And hold the gates of all their enemies.
Iddo, and Miriam, let me join your hands,
And be your hearts as one.
      Now, Hamel, come;
And bring thy loved one nearer to my couch,
That I may bless you with my latest breath.
Of worldly goods thou hast thy portion had,
And what remains thy brother justly claims.
Then take my blessing, it is all I have;
And may thy father's God, a hundredfold
Add to my largest wish. By Him endowed,
Thou shalt be doubly rich. Thou hast from me
But little need of wealth, in lands or gold;
For, with her hand, thy own sweet Esther brings—
As a fair portion, with her father's name—
Enough of both; while her pure virtue claims

To be for thee a rich inheritance.
Then take her hand, and plight your mutual troth
In vows of love. And may th' Eternal ear,
That now regards thy words, be open e'er
To thy requests; and that All-seing eye
Which now beholds, watch o'er thy every path,
And stretch the arm of His protecting care
Around thy way. And may thy arm be strong,
And thy wide quiver full of polished shafts.
And let thy strength be counted by thy sons,
Who, as a mighty army, shall prevail,
And rear their heads like Bashan's sturdy oaks,
And spread the arms of their protection o'er
The minor tribes. Hamel, my darling son!
My youngest, best belov'd;—a light that streamed
Across the dusky horizon of life,
To cheer the twilight of my mortal sphere—
May thy light ever shine, and brighter grow,
As of the just unto the perfect day.
Take now thy bride, and treasure in thy heart,
The pure, unselfish love, she gives to thee.

. . . . . .

Lift up my head—I hear the chariot wheels:
The flaming steeds I see. He comes! He comes!
I haste—I haste away. Sons, friends, good bye.

Chorus of Friends.

Thy happy soul has passed the bounds of Time,
And in Elijah's car is upwards borne,
To glory's highest realms.   Thou dost rejoice,
Now, in thy Father's love.—O! boundless love!—
And, in His presence, art for ever glad.
" It was meet we should make merry and be glad :
" For this thy son was dead, and is alive again;
" Was lost, but now is found."

JOHN T. BEER,

CORNER OF BOAR LANE, BRIGGATE,

LEEDS,

Begs to invite the attention of his numerous Patrons to the

CHOICE AND SELECT STOCK

OF FASHIONABLE

HOME-MADE CLOTHING,

Always to be seen at his Establishment, where

PRICE, QUALITY, AND STYLE,

COMBINE IN FORMING

A novel and attractive Feature of Business.

THE ORDER DEPARTMENT,

Connected with this Establishment,

WILL BE FOUND TO UNITE ALL THE EXCELLENCE OF A

FIRST CLASS TRADE,

WITH THE STRICTEST ECONOMY IN PRICE,

Being personally superintended by the Proprietor, whose thoroughly practical and long experience, is a safe guarantee for the complete efficiency of this important branch of the business.

THE STOCK OF MATERIAL

ON HAND, IS ALWAYS OF THE

NEWEST AND BEST DESCRIPTION,

COMPRISING A GREAT VARIETY IN

West of England, Scotch, and Yorkshire Manufacture,

Which will be made up by first class Workmen, who are liberally remunerated for their labour.

THE BUSINESS

INCLUDES

BROAD CLOTHS, WEST AND YORKSHIRE;

DOESKINS, BLACK AND COLOURED;

TWEEDS, OF EVERY DESCRIPTION:

READY-MADE CLOTHING;

WATERPROOF COATS AND OVERALLS;

HATS, AND MOURNING BANDS;

BRACES, in great variety.

NECK TIES, SCARFS, MUFFLERS;

Travelling Rugs, Umbrellas, &c.

JOHN T. BEER,

TAILOR,

CLOTHING MANUFACTURER & HATTER,

CORNER OF BOAR LANE,

BRIGGATE, LEEDS.

Every purchaser to the amount of £1 and upwards, will be entitled to receive a copy of this book.

www.ingramcontent.com/pod-product-compliance
Lightning Source LLC
Chambersburg PA
CBHW031503160426
43195CB00010BB/1091